MW00475049

HBR Guide to
Your
Professional
Growth

Harvard Business Review Guides

Arm yourself with the advice you need to succeed on the job, from the most trusted brand in business. Packed with how-to essentials from leading experts, the HBR Guides provide smart answers to your most pressing work challenges.

The titles include:

HBR Guide to Being More Productive

HBR Guide to Better Business Writing

HBR Guide to Building Your Business Case

HBR Guide to Buying a Small Business

HBR Guide to Coaching Employees

HBR Guide to Data Analytics Basics for Managers

HBR Guide to Delivering Effective Feedback

HBR Guide to Emotional Intelligence

HBR Guide to Finance Basics for Managers

HBR Guide to Getting the Right Work Done

HBR Guide to Leading Teams

HBR Guide to Making Every Meeting Matter

HBR Guide to Managing Stress at Work

HBR Guide to Managing Up and Across

HBR Guide to Negotiating

HBR Guide to Office Politics

HBR Guide to Performance Management

HBR Guide to Persuasive Presentations

HBR Guide to Project Management

HBR Guide to
Your Professional Growth

HARVARD BUSINESS REVIEW PRESS

Boston, Massachusetts

Copyright 2019 Harvard Business School Publishing Corporation

All rights reserved

Printed in the United States of America

10 9 8 7 6 5 4

No part of this publication may be reproduced, stored in or introduced into a retrieval system, or transmitted, in any form, or by any means (electronic, mechanical, photocopying, recording, or otherwise), without the prior permission of the publisher. Requests for permission should be directed to permissions@hbsp.harvard.edu, or mailed to Permissions, Harvard Business School Publishing, 60 Harvard Way, Boston, Massachusetts 02163.

The web addresses referenced in this book were live and correct at the time of the book's publication but may be subject to change.

Library of Congress Cataloging-in-Publication data is forthcoming.

ISBN: 9781633695986

eISBN: 9781633695993

The paper used in this publication meets the requirements of the American National Standard for Permanence of Paper for Publications and Documents in Libraries and Archives Z39.48-1992

What You'll Learn

No one will pay as close attention to your growth and development as you. Whether you're lucky enough to work for an organization that cultivates a learning mindset or if only a handful of stars get all the heat and light when it comes to professional development, you are the best person to build and monitor your own curriculum. And increasingly in today's organizations, the success of your career lies in *your* hands.

Without an HR specialist or a personal coach to guide you, how can you continue to learn, grow, stay relevant, and evolve into your best self at work? The process of mapping out your own development plan begins with understanding your strengths and weaknesses, gathering and distilling meaningful feedback, setting goals for yourself beyond your job duties, identifying and acquiring new skills, and nurturing your curiosity. Even if you're undecided on the long-term shape of your career, you can establish a course to acquire and maintain the skills you'll need to close the gap between where you are and where you'd like to be.

This guide will help you set a goal and chart the steps to take to achieve it, whether you're new to the workforce, at a turning point in your career, or looking to push yourself to the next level. You'll learn to:

- Identify and address gaps in your knowledge or skills

- Gather, interpret, and act on constructive feedback

- Develop or nurture a growth mindset

- Make time to learn by figuring out what to stop doing

- Evaluate educational opportunities from formal business degrees to online courses

- Set new goals—regularly—to keep learning

- Talk to your boss about making positive changes to your job

- Recognize when it's time for a new challenge

Contents

Contents

SECTION THREE

Set Goals for Yourself

SECTION FOUR

Become a Better Learner

Contents

SECTION FIVE

Gain New Skills

Set a Vision for Your Career

Only you can define success for yourself

CHAPTER 1

Reaching Your Potential

by Robert Steven Kaplan

IDEA IN BRIEF

Despite racking up impressive accomplishments, you feel frustrated with your career—convinced you should be achieving more. You may even wish you had chosen a different career altogether.

These feelings often stem from a common error: buying into others' definitions of success. To reach your potential, Kaplan suggests taking a deeply personal look at how *you* define success:

Reprinted from *Harvard Business Review*, July 2008 (product #R0807C).

Begin by recognizing that managing your career is *your* responsibility. Then, follow these three steps:

- **Know yourself** by identifying your strengths and weaknesses and the activities you truly enjoy doing.

- **Excel** at the activities critical to success in your desired role.

- **Demonstrate character and leadership** by putting the interests of your company and colleagues ahead of your own.

IDEA IN PRACTICE

Kaplan offers these guidelines for reaching your potential at work.

Know yourself

Write down your 2–3 greatest strengths and weaknesses. If (like most people) you struggle with identifying key weaknesses, solicit the views of people (peers, direct reports, trusted friends) who will tell you the brutal truth. Ask for very specific feedback ("How well do I listen?" "What is my leadership style?"). Be receptive to the input you receive.

Then figure out what you truly enjoy doing. What's your dream job? Resist the lure of a hot field: If you go into it without a strong enthusiasm for the actual work, you may waste a number of years before you admit it's the wrong job for you. Once you've chosen your ideal job, you'll have to start from scratch. But choosing a field you love gives you strength to weather the inevitable setbacks and long hours needed to reach your full potential in any career.

Excel at critical activities

Identify the 3–4 activities essential for success in your desired or current role. Then develop a plan for excelling in these activities.

> *Example:* A new division head at a large industrial company was struggling to grow sales and profits. Through interviews with staff and customers, he concluded that success in his business hinged on developing close relationships with top customers' purchasing managers, putting the right people in critical leadership positions, and staying at the cutting edge of product innovation. He began delegating activities less central to success so he could focus on raising the bar on the three success factors he had identified. Sales and profits improved.

Demonstrate character and leadership

Character and leadership make the difference between good and great performance. To demonstrate *character*:

- Put the interests of your company and colleagues ahead of your own, doing things for others without regard to what's in it for you.

- Adopt an owner's mindset, asking yourself what you would do if you were the ultimate decision maker.

- Be willing to make recommendations that will benefit your organization's overall performance, possibly to the detriment of your own unit. Trust that you'll eventually be rewarded.

To exhibit *leadership*, speak up—even when you're expressing an unpopular view. Your superiors desperately want dissenting opinions so they can make better choices. If you play it safe instead of asserting your heartfelt opinions, you may hit a plateau in your career.

Ambitious professionals often spend a substantial amount of time thinking about strategies that will help them achieve greater levels of success. They strive for a more impressive job title, higher compensation, and responsibility for more sizable revenues, profits, and numbers of employees. Their definitions of success are often heavily influenced by family, friends, and colleagues.

Yet many ultimately find that, despite their efforts and accomplishments, they lack a true sense of professional satisfaction and fulfillment. During my career with Goldman Sachs, as well as over the past few years of teaching and coaching managers and MBA students at Harvard Business School, I have met a surprisingly large number of impressive executives who expressed deep frustration with their careers. They looked back and felt that they should have achieved more or even wished that they had chosen a different career altogether.

Consider a very successful research analyst at a large securities firm who came to see me because he was discouraged with his career progress. This was particularly ironic because he was well known, highly regarded (ranked number one in his industry sector), and well compensated. He told me that, after 10 years, he was tired of his job, disliked his boss, and felt he had no potential for further upward mobility. Most of all, he had always wanted to be an investment manager, but he had started out as an analyst and never really reassessed his career path. He felt trapped. He feared losing his stature and didn't want to let anyone down, but at the same time he didn't want to keep doing what he was doing.

As we talked, he wondered if he'd been so busy trying to reach specific milestones and impress other people that he'd lost sight of what he really enjoyed doing. The truth was that he loved analyzing stocks and assessing management teams, but he also wanted to have the responsibility for making the actual investment decisions and then be held accountable for the results. I encouraged him to take action and speak to a number of investment firms (including his current employer) about a career change. After doing this, he ultimately was offered and accepted a portfolio manager position in the asset management division of his current firm. He learned that his firm's leaders wanted to retain him regardless of job description and that they were quite surprised to find out he wanted to be on the investment side of the business. He has since become a

CAREER COUNSEL: FOLLOW YOUR OWN PATH

Reaching your potential requires introspection and certain proactive behaviors—but it starts with a basic philosophy, or "rules of the road."

1. *Managing your career is 100% your responsibility, and you need to act accordingly.* Many promising professionals expect their superiors to mentor them, give them thoughtful coaching, provide them with challenging opportunities, and generally steer their development. Such a passive approach is likely to derail you at some point. While your superiors will play a role, your career is your own.

2. *Be wary of conventional wisdom.* It's almost always wrong—for you. Hopping on the bandwagon may feel good initially but often leads to

superb investment manager, and although he wishes he'd stepped back and reexamined his career years earlier, he's thrilled that he made the switch while there was "still time."

If you are experiencing similar feelings of frustration or even regret about the direction of your career, this article is intended to help you examine the question, "Am I reaching my potential?" This is not the same as asking, "How do I rise to the top?" or "How can I be successful in my career?" Rather, it's about taking a very personal painful regrets years later. To reach your potential, you must filter out peer pressure and popular opinion; assess your own passions, skills, and convictions; and then be courageous enough to act on them.

3. *Have faith that, although justice may not prevail at any given point in time, it should generally prevail over time.* When you do suffer an injustice, you need to be willing to step back and objectively assess your own role in these events. That mindset will help you learn from inevitable setbacks and eventually bounce back. It will also help you stay focused on issues you can control as well as bolster your determination to act like the ultimate decision maker.

look at how *you* define success in your heart of hearts and then finding *your* path to get there.

To do that, you must step back and reassess your career—starting with the recognition that managing it is your responsibility. Too many people feel like victims in their careers, when in fact they have a substantial degree of control. Seizing control requires you to take a fresh look at your behavior in three main areas: knowing yourself, excelling at critical tasks, and demonstrating character and leadership.

Knowing Yourself

Taking responsibility for your career starts with an accurate assessment of your current skills and performance. Can you write down your two or three greatest strengths and your two or three most significant weaknesses? While most people can detail their strengths, they often struggle to identify key weaknesses. This exercise involves meaningful reflection and, almost always, requires soliciting the views of people who will tell you the brutal truth. Unfortunately, you often can't count on your boss to accurately assess your strengths or to be willing to confront you with what you're doing wrong. It's up to you to take control of this process by seeking coaching, asking for very specific feedback, and being receptive to input from a wide variety of people at various levels within your organization. This gathering of feedback needs to be an ongoing process because, as your career progresses, you will face new challenges and demands.

Recently I met with a division head of a large professional services firm. Though he'd been a rising star for several years, he felt he'd begun to stagnate. His direct reports and his CEO no longer seemed engaged and enthusiastic in their dealings with him, and he didn't know why. In our discussions, he was able to specifically describe his strengths, but when I asked about his weaknesses, he gave me fairly generic responses, such as "Maybe I'm too impatient" and "I need to raise my profile." When I pressed him about feedback from his boss, he still struggled to identify even one specific weakness. I sent him off on an assignment: interview at least five colleagues and subordinates.

He returned a few weeks later with several "surprises." He'd heard, for example, that while he was detail-oriented and decisive, he micromanaged, had a dictatorial style, and failed to listen. Armed with these insights, he sought coaching, started working on his flaws, and began regularly soliciting feedback from his colleagues and subordinates. A year later he reported that his effectiveness had improved as a result of these ongoing efforts, and he was once again feeling confident and optimistic about his career.

This type of initiative takes time, humility, and a willingness to confront weaknesses, fears, and blind spots that many of us would rather ignore. But I never cease to be impressed by the capacity of people to change and improve once they recognize their shortcomings as well as their strengths.

Of course, getting others to tell you where you're falling short isn't easy—particularly if they're your subordinates. It must be done in one-on-one conversations, and you need to give potential coaches time to learn that you're sincere. When your employees see you actually act on their feedback, they are likely to become more proactive in offering advice, because they know you value their input. Your subordinates and colleagues will also feel they have a stake in your success and that of your unit—which will make them more likely to enjoy working with you.

Once you have a grip on your strengths and weaknesses, your next challenge is to figure out what you truly enjoy doing. What's your dream job? How well does it match what you currently do? Many people either don't know what their passions are or are so focused on the views of their peers that they drift into the wrong career. I was recently approached by an MBA student who wanted advice on whether to go work for a hedge fund, a private equity firm, or an investment bank. When asked whether he had an interest in financial markets, he quickly said no. He wasn't even sure about the key tasks that each of those jobs would entail. When asked what he would do if he had $10 million in the bank, however, his answer was very clear: pursue a career in the music industry. He was a concert-level musician and loved the music business. Once he recognized how much he had been swayed by his fellow students' bias toward the lucrative financial services industry, he realized he needed to rethink his choices.

The conventional wisdom about the attractiveness of various careers changes constantly. Twenty-five years ago the medical and legal professions were considered financially rewarding and socially desirable. Today, a number of doctors and lawyers are frustrated in their jobs and realize that they might have based their career choices excessively on the views of their peers and popular opinion, instead of on whether they would actually love the work. Hedge funds and private equity are today's hot fields, but people who go into them without a strong enthusiasm for the actual tasks may find themselves starting from scratch a few years down the line. Loving what you do gives you the strength to weather personal setbacks, overcome adversity, face and address your weaknesses, and work the long hours typically needed to reach your full potential.

Excelling at Critical Tasks

It's very difficult to succeed if you don't excel at the tasks that are central to your chosen enterprise. That sounds painfully simple, but many executives fail to identify the three or four most important activities that lead to success in their job or business. If you're a medical researcher, the three keys are likely to be conducting cutting-edge research, getting published, and fund-raising. If you manage a large sales force, the crucial tasks might be attracting, retaining, and developing outstanding salespeople; customer segmentation; and client relationship management. If you're assessing a potential job move, you need to know what will drive success in the new position and, then, ask yourself whether you enjoy those key tasks. In your current job, identifying critical tasks helps you determine how to spend your time and develop your skills.

Promising leaders sometimes lose sight of this connection. Not long ago, a new division head at a large industrial company told me that he was struggling to grow sales and profits. He complained that he was spending too much time fighting fires and didn't have enough hours in the day. When I asked him to identify the three main drivers of success in his business, he realized that he wasn't sure. He spent the next several weeks interviewing staff and customers, and concluded that success in his business depended on developing close relationships with the purchasing managers at each of his top 25 customers, putting the right people in critical sales and manufacturing leadership positions, and staying

13

at the cutting edge of product innovation. He also realized that his division was performing poorly in all three areas.

He proceeded to clear his calendar, force himself to delegate tasks that were less central to success, and focus on raising the bar in each of these areas. Six months later he reported that he had replaced a number of executives—including the sales manager and head of product development—and created an executive committee that met weekly to discuss critical business issues. He also reported that he'd become much more disciplined in matching his priorities (and those of his leadership team) with the keys to success for the business. Sales and profits began to improve, and he felt confident that he would resume his upward career trajectory.

Demonstrating Character and Leadership

While seemingly amorphous, character and leadership often make the difference between good performance and great performance. One measure of character is the degree to which you put the interests of your company and colleagues ahead of your own. Excellent leaders are willing to do things for others without regard to what's in it for them. They coach and mentor. They have the mindset of an owner and figure out what they would do if they were the ultimate decision maker. They're willing to make a recommendation that would benefit the organization's overall performance, possibly to the detriment of their own unit. They have the courage to trust that they will eventually be rewarded, even if their actions may not be in their own short-term interest.

Being a leader also means being willing to speak up, even when you're expressing an unpopular view. CEOs' proposals often generate head nodding, even from people who secretly harbor serious reservations. In reality, most chief executives desperately want dissenting opinions so they can make better choices. While emerging leaders must use good judgment regarding the tone and timing of their dissent, they also need to be aware that they can hit a plateau by playing it safe when they should be asserting their heartfelt opinions.

One CEO recounted to me his regrets over a recent key hire. His top three reports had each interviewed the various job candidates and expressed no major concerns about the final choice. After the new hire was on board—and had begun to struggle—it came to light that two of the three senior managers had privately held significant reservations but concluded that the CEO's mind was made up and that speaking out was unwise. The CEO was furious. Though he recognized his own role in the mess (he vowed to more actively encourage dissent), he also lowered his opinion of the two executives who failed to express their views.

Otherwise confident executives sometimes overestimate the career risk of speaking up and meaningfully underestimate the risk of staying silent. I encourage people to develop various approaches to help them overcome this hesitancy: For example, I've counseled emerging executives to save their money to build financial security and to avoid getting too emotionally attached to their jobs. Though it may seem that you'll never find another great job, you have to have faith that there are many attractive opportunities outside your firm.

In some cases, I advise people to become experts in some specific business area in order to build their confidence. I also encourage people to spend more time deciding what they truly believe versus trying to guess what the boss might want to hear. At work, as in competitive sports, you must play with confidence and even a little abandon. I've talked to several executives whose finest moments came when they gathered their courage and confidently expressed disagreement with their boss and peers. To their surprise, they found that they were treated with more respect after these episodes.

Most outstanding CEOs value emerging executives who assert themselves out of genuine concern for what is best for the company. Doing the right thing is a reward in itself—psychologically in the short run and professionally in the longer run. Of course, this approach requires that you have some reasonable level of faith that justice will prevail. I have seldom seen people hurt their careers by speaking up and appropriately articulating a well-thought-out contrary position (even when it was unpopular). However, I have seen many bitter and confused people who stalled their careers by playing it safe.

Every rewarding career will bring ups and downs, bad days, bad weeks, and bad months. Everyone will face setbacks and discouraging situations. Some people abandon their plans when they hit one of these bumps. They lose their way and ultimately undermine their own performance—and the wound is all the more painful because it is self-inflicted. The advice in this article is intended to help you avoid such self-inflicted wounds. There's nothing anyone can do to prevent you from reaching your potential; the challenge is for you to identify your dream, develop the skills to get there, and exhibit character and leadership. Then, you need to have the courage to periodically reassess, make adjustments, and pursue a course that reflects who you truly are.

Robert Steven Kaplan is president and chief executive of the Federal Reserve Bank of Dallas. Previously, he was the senior associate dean for external relations and Martin Marshall Professor of Management Practice in Business Administration at Harvard Business School. He is the author of three books: *What You Really Need to Lead, What You're Really Meant to Do*, and *What to Ask the Person in the Mirror*, all published by Harvard Business Review Press.

CHAPTER 2

Developing a Strategy for a Life of Meaningful Labor

by Brian Fetherstonhaugh

In a world of constant disruption, both opportunity and uncertainty exist in the workplace. All of us need a new way of thinking about work and taking personal responsibility for our careers, which last 45 years and beyond.

Over the past three decades, I have been counseling and mentoring people and conducting research on the topic of career strategy. I've been struck by how many

---

Adapted from content posted on hbr.org, September 5, 2016 (product #H0341F).

people at all stages of life are extremely anxious about their career but have invested little time in creating a strategy for it. If you are one of those people, take the time to change that: Set aside a day to create a plan for pursuing the most purposeful and rewarding work possible. Whether you're a millennial, a Gen Xer, or a baby boomer, here are five actions you can take to get your career strategy rolling.

Calculate How Much Longer You'll Be Working $65 - 30 = 35y$

Most people vastly underestimate how long a career lasts, so do some simple math. Tally up how many years, days, and hours you expect to be working, even part-time. Hint: The current average retirement age in the United States is 65, but it's going up. Many are choosing—or needing—to work well into their seventies.

Figure Out What Career Stage You Are At

There are three major career stages, each lasting about 15 years. You'll need to adjust as you pass through them.

- **Stage one: start of career through midthirties.** Make this your time to discover, learn, and try different things. Sign up for some special assignments at work. Take an online course. Volunteer for a not-for-profit organization that might stretch your skills. Be open to opportunities inside and outside of your company if you believe they can accelerate your learning. You're sure to take a few wrong turns, but even mistakes and learning what you don't like are valuable.

- **Stage two: late thirties to early fifties.** This is your time to reach high by building on strengths and differentiating yourself from others. You'll want to find your sweet spot, which is the intersection of what you love, what you're good at, and what the world values.

- **Stage three: midfifties and beyond.** At age 50, you could easily have more than 20 years of work life left. Your work should be sustainable and keep a reasonable pace that could last for decades. One of your main areas of focus at this stage should be to stay fresh. Nobody wants to hire someone who is only concerned with the past. Stay relevant and well connected so that you can become a practitioner of "active wisdom" for years to come. Try some reverse mentoring—share some of your expertise with a younger colleague in exchange for what they know about today. Remain a lifelong learner. Read up on current technologies and emerging industries and think about how the principles and knowledge you have accumulated could be applied into the future.

Take Inventory of How Much "Career Fuel" You Have

The people who are most successful in the long term are those who have an abundant supply of what I call "career fuel": transportable skills, meaningful experiences, and enduring relationships.

Transportable skills include problem solving, being adept at persuading others, getting things done, and knowing how to take smart risks. These are skills you can carry with you from job to job, company to company, and industry to industry.

Meaningful experiences take us out of our comfort zone and make us more adaptable to changes in our job environment. Think travel, intense community service, launching products, or starting your own business.

Enduring relationships are perhaps the most powerful form of career fuel: the connections, experts, critical colleagues, and mentors who make a huge difference in your career progression.

Assess whether your fuel levels are growing, stagnating, or perhaps even declining. Ask yourself what you can do in the next year to replenish them. You don't always need to change jobs or industries to add fuel. Look for new pathways within your own organization through a special assignment, job rotation, expanded responsibilities, or structured training.

Grade Your Current Work Situation

Don't depend on your gut or how you feel late on a Friday evening to evaluate your job satisfaction. Get objective by asking these four questions: Are you learning? Are you having impact? Are you having fun? And, finally, are you being fairly rewarded?

Regarding the last one: Look at the full package of rewards, including salary, benefits, vacation, and workplace flexibility. Is it fair for what you are contributing to the organization? How does it compare to the going rate in the marketplace?

What do the answers to these questions show you? Could you boost some of the low ratings? Can they be fixed in your current situation, or should you look elsewhere?

Invest Your Time Wisely

Time is the currency of our lives, and how we spend it speaks volumes about what we think is important. Sketch a simple pie chart of how you have spent your time over the past couple of months, using categories such as work, family, community, health, and relaxation.

What does your pie chart say about how you're investing in yourself? What balance of work and play is sustainable for the journey ahead? Are you devoting enough time to the things that really make you happy, even in small doses? Should you adjust your time as you transition from one stage to another? Are you using your precious time to build fuel? How does your time portfolio relate to your answers to the job satisfaction questions?

A career is a long ride, and it's more than just work: It's a huge part of life. Take time to think strategically about your career journey. Only one person will be with you for the whole ride, and that's you. Don't just worry about it—take some action.

———————

Brian Fetherstonhaugh is global chief talent officer of The Ogilvy Group and the author of *The Long View: Career Strategies to Start Strong, Reach High, and Go Far* (Diversion Publishing, 2016).

CHAPTER 3

Think Strategically About Your Career Development

by Dorie Clark

Your boss or HR leadership simply doesn't have the time or bandwidth to properly think through how best to deploy your talents amid countless emails and meetings. Instead, we have to take control of our career planning to ensure we're positioning ourselves for long-term growth.

Here are four ways to become more strategic about the process.

Adapted from content posted on hbr.org, December 6, 2016 (product #H03BQF).

Force yourself to set aside time

When things get busy, time for strategic thinking is almost always the first to go. "Planning sessions" seem amorphous, and the ROI is uncertain. But going for months or years without regular introspection can lead you down a professional path you didn't intend to be on. Instead, force yourself to make time for strategic reflection. Just as you're more likely to go to the gym if you have plans to meet a workout buddy, you can use the same technique to enforce discipline around strategic thinking. Identify several trusted colleagues and start a mastermind group to meet regularly, discuss big-picture goals, and hold each other accountable for meeting those goals. Having others whom you trust challenge your thinking can open ideas and possibilities you hadn't previously considered.

Get clear on your next steps

Getting clarity around your professional goals—such as being promoted to senior vice president, starting your own business, or running the Asia-Pacific region—is only the first step. The place where many of us fall down is identifying the pathway to get from here to there. Try "pre-writing" your résumé. Put yourself five years into the future and write your résumé as you envision it, including your new title and exact job responsibilities. The trick is that you also have to fill in the intervening five years, which prompts you to reflect on what specific skills you'll need to develop in the interim, what degrees or accreditations you may need to earn, and what promotional path you'll need to pursue in order to get there. Understanding that encourages reflection and ensures that you're taking the right steps. Say a master's degree is required for a position you want in three years—it's time to start researching and applying to programs now.

Invest in deep work

It can be tempting to invest your time the same way everyone else does—putting in face time at the office, or racing to respond to emails the fastest. At lower levels, that might mark employees as "go-getters." But as you ascend in the organization, the ability to jump higher and faster becomes less important. Instead, what marks you as successful over time is creating in-depth, valuable projects—whether that's writing a book or a brilliant new piece of code, spearheading the launch of a promising product, or undertaking a meaningful initiative, like reorganizing the company's performance review system. That involves a shift from staccato, reactive work into more self-directed, long-term projects ("deep work," as author and professor Cal Newport puts it). Many of us don't seek out this work, as there's no immediate ROI, but the long-term benefits and recognition are substantial.

Build your external reputation

A study by Wharton professor Matthew Bidwell showed that external hires into a company get paid 18%–20% more than internal workers who are promoted into similar jobs. (Gratingly, they also perform worse for the first two years.) That's patently unjust, but it points to an important truth: People are often taken for granted inside their own organizations. That doesn't mean you should jump ship every few years. But it does indicate that, even if you'd like to stay at the same company, it's important to cultivate a strong external reputation so that you have opportunities if you want them, and to remind your boss and colleagues that your abilities are sought after and appreciated by others. Blogging for industry journals, applying to speak at conferences, and taking on a leadership role in your professional association are all great ways to stay visible in your field—both to outsiders and to those inside your company who need to be reminded of your talents.

Taking time to think about your career development is obviously important, but it's almost never urgent, so many of us fail to take action, year after year. By focusing on these four steps, you can begin to carve out time to be more deliberate and lay the groundwork for the job you want—five years from now, and beyond.

Dorie Clark is a marketing strategist and professional speaker who teaches at Duke University's Fuqua School of Business. She is the author of *Entrepreneurial You* (Harvard Business Review Press, 2017), *Reinventing You* (Harvard Business Review Press, 2013), and *Stand Out* (Portfolio, 2015).

Assess Yourself and Gather Feedback

CHAPTER 4

Career Self-Assessment Worksheet

To manage your career effectively, you need to know yourself well. Identifying your strengths and gaps can help you know where to start when asking for the learning opportunities and support you need. This brief self-assessment will help you begin to capture your skills and interests and unearth areas to explore as you begin to solicit feedback from others. When you know what you do well—and what you most enjoy—it's easier to identify opportunities that allow you to deliver your best effort and cultivate a fulfilling career.

Adapted from Career Management module, Harvard ManageMentor.

Instructions

Use the following questions to help you think through your developmental needs and goals. Periodically returning to this assessment will help you understand where you are—and where you'd like to go—as your career path evolves.

1. What's the overall fit between your current position and your interests, values, and skills?

2. What is your overall level of satisfaction with your current position?

3. What do you think others would say are your strengths?

4. What do you think others would say are your gaps?

5. What do *you* consider to be your top five skills (that is, those where you have the most proficiency)?

6. Of your top skills, which ones do you most enjoy using?

7. What are the top two or three skills you need or want to learn in order to grow in your job, advance to the next level, or seek a new job?

8. What are your key transferable skills—those skills that are not just job-specific but that can be applied to work in many positions (such as basic computer skills, negotiation skills, financial analysis)?

9. What are your long-term career goals?

10. With your long-term career goals in mind, what are your short-term career-development goals? Where would you like to be 6 to 12 months from now?

11. What are some developmental opportunities you can take advantage of?

CHAPTER 5

What Self-Awareness Really Is (and How to Cultivate It)

by Tasha Eurich

Self-awareness seems to have become the latest management buzzword—and for good reason. Research suggests that when we see ourselves clearly, we are more confident and more creative. We make sounder decisions, build stronger relationships, and communicate more effectively. We're less likely to lie, cheat, and steal. We are better workers who get more promotions. And we're

---

Adapted from content posted on hbr.org, January 4, 2018 (product #H042DK).

more effective leaders with more satisfied employees and more profitable companies.

As an organizational psychologist and executive coach, I've had a ringside seat to the power of leadership self-awareness for nearly 15 years. I've also seen how attainable this skill is. Yet, when I first began to delve into the research on self-awareness, I was surprised by the striking gap between the science and the practice of self-awareness. All things considered, we knew surprisingly little about improving this critical skill.

Four years ago, my team of researchers and I embarked on a large-scale scientific study of self-awareness. In 10 separate investigations with nearly 5,000 participants, we examined what self-awareness really is, why we need it, and how we can increase it.

Our research revealed many surprising roadblocks, myths, and truths about what self-awareness is and what it takes to improve it. We've found that even though most people *believe* they're self-aware, self-awareness is a truly rare quality: We estimate that only 10%–15% of the people we studied actually fit the criteria. Three findings in particular stood out, and are helping us develop practical guidance for how leaders can learn to see themselves more clearly.

There Are Two Types of Self-Awareness

For the last 50 years, researchers have used varying definitions of self-awareness. For example, some see it as the ability to monitor our inner world, whereas others label it as a temporary state of self-consciousness. Still others

describe it as the difference between how we see ourselves and how others see us. So before we could focus
on how to improve self-awareness, we needed to synthe-
size these findings and create an overarching definition.

Across the studies we examined, two broad categories of self-awareness kept emerging. The first, which we
dubbed *internal self-awareness*, represents how clearly
we see our own values, passions, aspirations, fit with
our environment, reactions (including thoughts, feelings, behaviors, strengths, and weaknesses), and impact
on others. We've found that internal self-awareness is
associated with higher job and relationship satisfaction,
personal and social control, and happiness; it is nega-
tively related to anxiety, stress, and depression.

The second category, *external self-awareness*, means
understanding how other people view us, in terms of
those same factors listed above. Our research shows that
people who know how others see them are more skilled
at showing empathy and taking others' perspectives. For
leaders who see themselves as their employees do, their
employees tend to have a better relationship with them,
feel more satisfied with them, and see them as more effective in general.

It's easy to assume that being high on one type of
awareness would mean being high on the other. But our
research has found virtually no relationship between
them. As a result, we identify four leadership archetypes,
each with a different set of opportunities to improve, in
figure 5-1. When it comes to internal and external self-
awareness, it's tempting to value one over the other. But
leaders must actively work on both seeing themselves

FIGURE 5-1

The four self-awareness archetypes

This 2×2 maps internal self-awareness (how well you know yourself) against external self-awareness (how well you understand how others see you).

	Low external self-awareness	High external self-awareness
High internal self-awareness	**INTROSPECTORS** They're clear on who they are but don't challenge their own views or search for blind spots by getting feedback from others. This can harm their relationships and limit their success.	**AWARE** They know who they are, what they want to accomplish, and seek out and value others' opinions. This is where leaders begin to fully realize the true benefits of self-awareness.
Low internal self-awareness	**SEEKERS** They don't yet know who they are, what they stand for, or how their teams see them. As a result, they might feel stuck or frustrated with their performance and relationships.	**PLEASERS** They can be so focused on appearing a certain way to others that they could be overlooking what matters to them. Over time, they tend to make choices that aren't in service of their own success and fulfillment.

Source: Dr. Tasha Eurich

clearly *and* getting feedback to understand how others see them. The highly self-aware people we interviewed were actively focused on balancing the scale.

Take Jeremiah, a marketing manager. Early in his career, he focused primarily on internal self-awareness—for example, deciding to leave his career in accounting to pursue his passion for marketing. But when he had the chance to get candid feedback during a company training, he realized that he wasn't focused enough on how he was showing up. Jeremiah has since placed an equal importance on both types of self-awareness, which he believes has helped him reach a new level of success and fulfillment.

Self-awareness isn't one truth. It's a delicate balance of two distinct, even competing, viewpoints.

Experience and Power Hinder Self-Awareness

Contrary to popular belief, studies have shown that people don't always learn from experience, that expertise doesn't help people root out false information, and that seeing ourselves as highly experienced can keep us from doing our homework, seeking disconfirming evidence, and questioning our assumptions.

And just as experience can lead to a false sense of confidence about our performance, it can also make us overconfident about our level of self-knowledge. For example, one study found that more experienced managers were less accurate in assessing their leadership effectiveness compared with less experienced managers.

Similarly, the more power a leader holds, the more likely they are to overestimate their skills and abilities. One study of more than 3,600 leaders across a variety of roles and industries found that, relative to lower-level leaders, higher-level leaders more significantly overvalued their skills (compared with others' perceptions). In fact, this pattern existed for 19 of the 20 competencies the researchers measured, including emotional self-awareness, accurate self-assessment, empathy, trustworthiness, and leadership performance.

Researchers have proposed two primary explanations for this phenomenon. First, by virtue of their level, senior leaders simply have fewer people above them who can provide candid feedback. Second, the more power a leader wields, the less comfortable people will be to give them constructive feedback, for fear it will hurt their careers. Business professor James O'Toole has added that, as someone's power grows, their willingness to listen shrinks, either because they think they know more than their employees or because seeking feedback will come at a cost.

But this doesn't have to be the case. One analysis showed that the most successful leaders, as rated by 360-degree reviews of leadership effectiveness, counteract this tendency by seeking frequent critical feedback (from bosses, peers, employees, their board, and so on). They become more self-aware in the process and come to be seen as more effective by others.

Likewise, in our interviews, we found that people who improved their external self-awareness did so by seeking out feedback from *loving critics*—that is, people who have their best interests in mind *and* are willing to tell them the truth. To ensure they don't overreact or overcorrect based on one person's opinion, they also gut-check difficult or surprising feedback with others.

Introspection Doesn't Always Improve Self-Awareness

It's also widely assumed that introspection—examining the causes of our own thoughts, feelings, and behaviors—improves self-awareness. After all, what better way to know ourselves than by reflecting on why we are the way we are?

Yet one of the most surprising findings of our research is that people who are introspective are *less* self-aware and report worse job satisfaction and well-being. Other research has shown similar patterns.

The problem with introspection isn't that it is categorically ineffective—it's that most people are doing it incorrectly. To understand this, let's look at arguably the most common introspective question: *Why?* We ask this when trying to understand our emotions (*Why do I like employee A so much more than employee B?*), or our behavior (*Why did I fly off the handle with that employee?*), or our attitudes (*Why am I so against this deal?*).

As it turns out, *why?* is a surprisingly ineffective self-awareness question. Research has shown that we simply do not have access to many of the unconscious thoughts, feelings, and motives we're searching for. And because so much is trapped outside our conscious awareness, we tend to invent answers that *feel* true but are often wrong. For example, after an uncharacteristic outburst at an employee, a new manager may jump to the conclusion that it happened because she isn't cut out for management, when the real reason was a bad case of low blood sugar.

Consequently, the problem with asking *why* isn't just how wrong we are, but how confident we are that we are right. The human mind rarely operates in a rational fashion, and our judgments are seldom free from bias. We tend to pounce on whatever insights we find, without questioning their validity or value, we ignore contradictory evidence, and we force our thoughts to conform to our initial explanations.

Another negative consequence of asking *why*—especially when trying to explain an undesired outcome—is that it invites unproductive negative thoughts. In our research, we've found that people who are very introspective are also more likely to get caught in ruminative patterns. For example, if an employee who receives a bad performance review asks, *Why did I get such a bad rating?*, they're likely to arrive at an explanation focused on their fears, shortcomings, or insecurities, rather than a rational assessment of their strengths and weaknesses. (For this reason, frequent self-analyzers are more depressed and anxious and experience poorer well-being.)

So if *why* isn't the right introspective question, is there a better one? My research team scoured hundreds of pages of interview transcripts with highly self-aware people to see if they approached introspection differently. Indeed, there was a clear pattern: Although the word *why* appeared fewer than 150 times, the word *what* appeared more than 1,000 times.

Therefore, to increase productive self-insight and decrease unproductive rumination, we should ask *what?*, not *why? What* questions help us stay objective, future-focused, and empowered to act on our new insights.

Consider Jose, an entertainment industry veteran we interviewed, who hated his job. Where many would have gotten stuck thinking "Why do I feel so terrible?" he asked, "What are the situations that make me feel terrible, and what do they have in common?" He realized that he'd never be happy in that career, and it gave him the courage to pursue a new and far more fulfilling one in wealth management.

Similarly, Robin, a customer service leader who was new to her job, needed to understand a piece of negative feedback she'd gotten from an employee. Instead of asking, "Why did you say this about me?" Robin inquired, "What are the steps I need to take in the future to do a better job?" This helped them move to solutions rather than focusing on the unproductive patterns of the past.

A final case is Paul, who told us about learning that the business he'd recently purchased was no longer profitable. At first, all he could ask himself was "Why wasn't I able to turn things around?" But he quickly realized that he didn't have the time or energy to beat himself up—he had to figure out what to do next. He started asking, "What do I need to do to move forward in a way that minimizes the impact to our customers and employees?" He created a plan, and was able to find creative ways to do as much good for others as possible while winding down the business. When all that was over, he challenged himself to articulate what he learned from the experience—his answer both helped him avoid similar mistakes in the future and helped others learn from them, too.

These qualitative findings have been bolstered by others' quantitative research. In one study, psychologists J. Gregory Hixon and William Swann gave a group of undergraduates negative feedback on a test of their "sociability, likability and interestingness." They gave some students time to think about *why* they were the kind of person they were, while they asked others to think about *what* kind of person they were. When the researchers had them evaluate the accuracy of the feedback, the *why* students spent their energy rationalizing and denying what they'd learned, and the *what* students were more open to this new information and how they might learn from it. Hixon and Swann's rather bold conclusion was that "[t]hinking about why one is the way one is may be no better than not thinking about one's self at all."

Leaders who focus on building both internal and external self-awareness, who seek honest feedback from loving critics, and who ask *what* instead of *why* can learn to see themselves more clearly—and reap the many rewards that increased self-knowledge delivers. And no matter how much progress we make, there's always more to learn. That's one of the things that makes the journey to self-awareness so exciting.

Tasha Eurich, PhD, is an organizational psychologist, researcher, and *New York Times* bestselling author. She is the principal of The Eurich Group, a boutique executive development firm that helps companies—from startups to the *Fortune* 100—succeed by improving the effectiveness of their leaders and teams. Her newest book, *Insight*, delves into the connection between self-awareness and success in the workplace.

CHAPTER 6

Why You Should Make Time for Self-Reflection (Even If You Hate Doing It)

by Jennifer Porter

When people find out I'm an executive coach, they often ask who my toughest clients are. Inexperienced leaders? Senior leaders who think they know everything? Leaders who bully and belittle others? Leaders who shirk responsibility?

Adapted from content posted on hbr.org, March 21, 2017 (product #H03JNJ).

The answer is none of the above. The hardest leaders to coach are those who won't reflect—particularly leaders who won't reflect on *themselves.*

At its simplest, reflection is about careful thought. But the kind of reflection that's really valuable to leaders is more nuanced than that. The most useful reflection involves the conscious consideration and analysis of beliefs and actions for the purpose of learning. Reflection gives the brain an opportunity to pause amid the chaos, untangle and sort through observations and experiences, consider multiple possible interpretations, and create meaning. This meaning becomes learning, which can then inform future mindsets and actions. For leaders, this "meaning making" is crucial to their ongoing growth and development.

So, if reflection is so helpful, why don't many leaders do it? Leaders often:

- **Don't understand the process.** Many leaders don't know how to reflect. One executive I work with, Ken, shared recently that he had yet again not met his commitment to spend an hour on Sunday mornings reflecting. To help him get over this barrier, I suggested he take the next 30 minutes of our two-hour session and just quietly reflect and then we'd debrief it. After five minutes of silence, he said, "I guess I don't really know what you want me to do. Maybe that's why I haven't been doing it."

- **Don't like the process.** Reflection requires leaders to do a number of things they typically don't like to do: slow down, adopt a mindset of not knowing and curiosity, tolerate messiness and inefficiency, and take personal responsibility. The process can lead to valuable insights and even breakthroughs— and it can also lead to feelings of discomfort, vulnerability, defensiveness, and irritation.

- **Don't like the results.** When a leader takes time to reflect, she typically sees ways she was effective as well as things she could have done better. Most leaders quickly dismiss the noted strengths and dislike the noted weaknesses. Some become so defensive in the process that they don't learn anything, so the results are not helpful.

- **Have a bias toward action.** Like soccer goalies, many leaders have a bias toward action. A study of professional soccer goalies defending penalty kicks found that goalies who stay in the center of the goal, instead of lunging left or right, have a 33% chance of stopping the goal, and yet these goalies only stay in the center 6% of the time. The goalies just feel better when they do something. The same is true of many leaders. Reflection can feel like staying in the center of the goal and missing the action.

- **Can't see a good ROI.** From early roles, leaders are taught to invest where they can generate a positive ROI—results that indicate the contribution of time, talent, or money paid off. Sometimes it's hard to see an immediate ROI on reflection— particularly when compared with other uses of a leader's time.

If you've found yourself making these same excuses, you can become more reflective by practicing a few simple steps.

- **Identify some important questions.** But don't answer them yet. Here are some possibilities:

  - What are you avoiding?

  - How are you helping your colleagues achieve their goals?

  - How are you *not* helping or even hindering their progress?

  - How might you be contributing to your least enjoyable relationship at work?

  - How could you have been more effective in a recent meeting?

- **Select a reflection process that matches your preferences.** Many people reflect through writing in a journal. If that sounds terrible but talking with a colleague sounds better, consider that. As long as you're reflecting and not just chatting about the latest sporting event or complaining about a colleague, your approach is up to you. You can sit, walk, bike, or stand—alone or with a partner—or write, talk, or think.

- **Schedule time.** Most leaders are driven by their calendars. So, schedule your reflection time and then commit to keep it. And if you find yourself trying to skip it or avoid it, reflect on that.

- **Start small.** If an hour of reflection seems like too much, try 10 minutes. Harvard Business School professor Teresa Amabile and her colleagues found that the most significant driver of positive emotions and motivation at work was making progress on the tasks at hand. Set yourself up to make progress, even if it feels small.

- **Do it.** Go back to your list of questions and explore them. Be still. Think. Consider multiple perspectives. Look at the opposite of what you initially believe. Brainstorm. You don't have to like or agree with all of your thoughts—just think and examine your thinking.

- **Ask for help.** For most leaders, a lack of desire, time, experience, or skill can get in the way of reflection. Consider working with a colleague, therapist, or coach to help you make the time, listen carefully, be a thought partner, and hold you accountable.

Despite the challenges to reflection, the impact is clear. As Peter Drucker said: "Follow effective action with quiet reflection. From the quiet reflection, will come even more effective action."

Jennifer Porter is the managing partner of The Boda Group, a leadership and team development firm. She is a graduate of Bates College and the Stanford Graduate School of Business, an experienced operations executive, and an executive and team coach.

CHAPTER 7

Making Yourself Indispensable

by John H. Zenger, Joseph R. Folkman, and Scott Edinger

IDEA IN BRIEF

Good leaders can become exceptional by developing just a few of their strengths to the highest level—but not by merely doing more of the same. Instead, they need to engage in the business equivalent of cross-training—that is, to enhance complementary skills that will enable them to make fuller use of their strengths. For example, technical skills can become more effective when communication skills improve, making a leader's expertise

Reprinted from *Harvard Business Review*, October 2011 (product #R1110E).

more apparent and more accessible. Once a few of their strengths have reached the level of outstanding, leaders become indispensable to their organizations despite the weaknesses they may have.

A manager we'll call Tom was a midlevel sales executive at a *Fortune* 500 company. After a dozen or so years there, he was thriving—he made his numbers, he was well liked, he got consistently positive reviews. He applied for a promotion that would put him in charge of a high-profile worldwide product-alignment initiative, confident that he was the top candidate and that this was the logical next move for him, a seemingly perfect fit for his skills and ambitions. His track record was solid. He'd made no stupid mistakes or career-limiting moves, and he'd had no run-ins with upper management. He was stunned, then, when a colleague with less experience got the job. What was the matter?

As far as Tom could tell, nothing. Everyone was happy with his work, his manager assured him, and a recent 360-degree assessment confirmed her view. Tom was at or above the norm in every area, strong not only in delivering results but also in problem solving, strategic thinking, and inspiring others to top performance. "No need to reinvent yourself," she said. "Just keep doing what you're doing. Go with your strengths."

But how? Tom was at a loss. Should he think more strategically? Become even more inspiring? Practice problem solving more intently?

It's pretty easy and straightforward to improve on a weakness; you can get steady, measurable results through linear development—that is, by learning and practicing basic techniques. But the data from our decades of work with tens of thousands of executives all over the world has shown us that developing strengths is very different. Doing more of what you already do well yields only incremental improvement. To get appreciably better at it, you have to work on complementary skills—what we call *nonlinear* development. This has long been familiar to athletes as cross-training. A novice runner, for example, benefits from doing stretching exercises and running a few times a week, gradually increasing mileage to build up endurance and muscle memory. But an experienced marathoner won't get significantly faster merely by running ever longer distances. To reach the next level, he needs to supplement that regimen by building up complementary skills through weight training, swimming, bicycling, interval training, yoga, and the like.

So it is with leadership competencies. To move from good to much better, you need to engage in the business equivalent of cross-training. If you're technically adept, for instance, delving even more deeply into technical manuals won't get you nearly as far as honing a complementary skill such as communication, which will make your expertise more apparent and accessible to your coworkers.

In this article we provide a simple guide to becoming a far more effective leader. We will see how Tom identified his strengths, decided which one to focus on and which complementary skill to develop, and what the results were. The process is straightforward, but complements are not always obvious. So first we'll take a closer look at the leadership equivalent of cross-training.

The Interaction Effect

In cross-training, the combination of two activities produces an improvement—an *interaction effect*—substantially greater than either one can produce on its own. There's nothing mysterious here. Combining diet with exercise, for example, has long been known to be substantially more effective in losing weight than either diet or exercise alone.

In our previous research we found 16 differentiating leadership competencies that correlate strongly with positive business outcomes such as increased profitability, employee engagement, revenue, and customer satisfaction. Among those 16, we wondered, could we find pairs that would produce significant interaction effects?

We searched through our database of more than a quarter million 360-degree surveys of some 30,000 developing leaders for pairings that resulted in far higher scores on overall leadership effectiveness than either attribute did on its own. The results were unambiguous. Take, for example, the competencies "focuses on results" and "builds relationships." Only 14% of leaders who were reasonably strong (that is, scored in the 75th percentile) in focusing on results but less so in building relationships reached the extraordinary leadership level: the 90th percentile in overall leadership effectiveness. Similarly, only 12% of those who were reasonably strong in building relationships but less so in focusing on results reached that level. But when an individual performed well in both categories, something dramatic happened: Fully 72% of those in the 75th percentile in both categories reached the 90th percentile in overall leadership effectiveness.

We measured the degree of correlation between overall leadership effectiveness and all possible pairings of our 16 differentiating competencies to learn which pairings were the most powerful. We also matched our 16 competencies with other leadership skills and measured how those pairs correlated with overall leadership effectiveness. We discovered that each of the 16 has up to a dozen associated behaviors—which we call *competency companions*—that were highly correlated with leadership excellence when combined with the differentiating competency. (For a complete list of the competencies and their companions, see figure 7-1.)

Consider the main competency "displays honesty and integrity." How would a leader go about improving a relative strength in this area? By being more honest? (We've heard that answer to the question many times.) That's not particularly useful advice. If an executive were weak in this area, we could recommend various ways to improve: Behave more consistently, avoid saying one thing and doing another, follow through on stated commitments, and so on. But a leader with high integrity is most likely already doing those things.

Our competency-companion research suggests a practical path forward. For example, assertiveness is among the behaviors that when paired with honesty and integrity correlate most strongly with high levels of overall leadership effectiveness. We don't mean to imply

FIGURE 7-1

What skills will magnify my strengths?

Our research shows that 16 leadership competencies correlate strongly with positive business outcomes. Each of them has up to a dozen "competency companions" whose development will strengthen the core skill.

CHARACTER

Displays honesty and integrity

- Shows concern and consideration for others
- Is trustworthy
- Demonstrates optimism
- Is assertive
- Inspires and motivates others
- Deals well with ambiguity
- Is decisive
- Focuses on results

PERSONAL CAPABILITY

Exhibits technical/professional expertise

- Solves problems and analyzes issues
- Builds relationships and networks
- Communicates powerfully and broadly
- Pursues excellence
- Takes initiative
- Develops others
- Displays honesty and integrity
- Acts in the team's best interest

Solves problems and analyzes issues

- Takes initiative
- Is organized and good at planning
- Is decisive
- Innovates
- Wants to tackle challenges
- Develops strategic perspective
- Acts independently
- Has technical expertise
- Communicates powerfully and broadly

Innovates

- Is willing to take risks and challenge the status quo
- Supports others in risk taking
- Solves problems and analyzes issues
- Champions change
- Learns quickly from success and failure
- Develops strategic perspective
- Takes initiative

Practices self-development

- Listens
- Is open to others' ideas

56

- Respects others
- Displays honesty and integrity
- Inspires and motivates others
- Provides effective feedback and development
- Takes initiative
- Is willing to take risks and challenge the status quo

GETTING RESULTS

Focuses on results

- Is organized and good at planning
- Displays honesty and integrity
- Anticipates problems
- Sees desired results clearly
- Provides effective feedback and development
- Establishes stretch goals
- Is personally accountable
- Is quick to act
- Provides rewards and recognition
- Creates a high-performance team
- Marshals adequate resources
- Innovates

Establishes stretch goals

- Inspires and motivates others
- Is willing to take risks and challenge the status quo
- Gains the support of others
- Develops strategic perspective
- Champions change
- Is decisive
- Has technical and business expertise
- Focuses on results

Takes initiative

- Anticipates problems
- Emphasizes speed
- Is organized and good at planning
- Champions others
- Deals well with ambiguity
- Follows through
- Inspires and motivates others
- Establishes stretch goals
- Displays honesty and integrity

INTERPERSONAL SKILLS

Communicates powerfully and broadly

- Inspires and motivates others
- Develops strategic perspective
- Establishes stretch goals
- Deals effectively with the outside world
- Is trustworthy
- Involves others
- Translates messages for clarity
- Solves problems and analyzes issues
- Takes initiative
- Innovates
- Develops others

(continued)

57

FIGURE 7-1 *(contined)*

Inspires and motivates others

- Connects emotionally with others
- Establishes stretch goals
- Exhibits clear vision and direction
- Communicates powerfully and broadly
- Develops others
- Collaborates and fosters teamwork
- Nurtures innovation
- Takes initiative
- Champions change
- Is a strong role model

Builds relationships

- Collaborates and fosters teamwork
- Displays honesty and integrity
- Develops others
- Listens
- Communicates powerfully and broadly
- Provides rewards and recognition
- Practices inclusion and values diversity
- Demonstrates optimism
- Practices self-development

Develops others

- Practices self-development
- Shows concern and consideration for others
- Is motivated by the success of others
- Practices inclusion and values diversity
- Develops strategic perspective
- Provides effective feedback and development
- Inspires and motivates others
- Innovates
- Provides rewards and recognition
- Displays honesty and integrity

Collaborates and fosters teamwork

- Is trustworthy
- Builds relationships and networks

a causal relationship here: Assertiveness doesn't make someone honest, and integrity doesn't produce assertiveness. But if a highly principled leader learned to become more assertive, he might be more likely to speak up and act with the courage of his convictions, thus applying his strength more widely or frequently to become a more effective leader.

- Practices inclusion and values diversity
- Develops strategic perspective
- Establishes stretch goals
- Communicates powerfully and broadly
- Displays honesty and integrity
- Adapts to change
- Inspires and motivates others
- Develops others

LEADING CHANGE

Develops strategic perspective

- Focuses on customers
- Innovates
- Solves problems and analyzes issues
- Communicates powerfully and broadly
- Establishes stretch goals
- Demonstrates business acumen
- Champions change
- Inspires and motivates others

Champions change

- Inspires and motivates others
- Builds relationships and networks
- Develops others
- Provides rewards and recognition
- Practices inclusion and values diversity
- Innovates
- Focuses on results
- Is willing to take risks and challenge the status quo
- Develops strategic perspective

Connects the group to the outside world

- Develops broad perspective
- Develops strategic perspective
- Inspires and motivates others
- Has strong interpersonal skills
- Takes initiative
- Gathers and assimilates information
- Champions change
- Communicates powerfully and broadly

Our data suggest other ways in which a competency companion can reinforce a leadership strength. It might make the strength more apparent, as in the case of the technically strong leader who improves her ability to communicate. Or skills learned in developing the competency companion might be profitably applied to the main competency. A leader strong in innovativeness, for instance, might learn how to champion change, thus encouraging his team to achieve results in new and more creative ways.

Building Strengths, Step-by-Step

As a practical matter, cross-training for leadership skills is clear-cut: (1) Identify your strengths. (2) Choose a strength to focus on according to its importance to the organization and how passionately you feel about it. (3) Select a complementary behavior you'd like to enhance. (4) Develop it in a linear way.

Identify your strengths

Strengths can arguably be identified in a variety of ways. But we contend that in the context of effective leadership, your view of your own (or even some perfectly objective view, supposing one could be had) is less important than other people's, because leadership is all about your effect on others. That's why we start with a 360—as Tom did.

Ideally, you should go about this in a psychometrically valid way, through a formal process in which you and your direct reports, peers, and bosses anonymously complete questionnaires ranking your leadership attributes on a quantitative scale. You and they should also answer some qualitative, open-ended questions concerning your strengths, your fatal flaws (if any), and the relative importance of those attributes to the company. By "fatal flaws," we mean flaws so critical that they can overpower any strengths you have or may develop—flaws that can derail your career.

Not every organization is able or willing to conduct 360s for everyone. So if that's not feasible, you may be able to solicit qualitative data from your colleagues if—and this is a big caveat—you can make them feel comfortable enough to be honest in their feedback. You could create your own feedback form and ask people to return it anonymously. (See the sidebar "An Informal 360" for a suggested set of questions.) We have also seen earnest one-on-one conversations work for this purpose; if nothing else, they show your coworkers that you are genuinely interested in self-improvement. (Nevertheless, it's unlikely that anyone will tell you directly if you have fatal flaws.)

In interpreting the results, people commonly focus first on their lowest scores. But unless those are extremely low (in the 10th percentile), that's a mistake. (We have found that 20% of executives do typically discover such a critical problem in their 360s; if you're among them, you must fix the flaw, which you can do in a linear way.)

What makes leaders indispensable to their organizations, our data unmistakably shows, is not being good at many things but being uniquely outstanding at a few things. Such strengths allow a leader's inevitable weaknesses to be overlooked. The executives in our database who exhibited no profound (that is, in the 90th percentile) strengths scored only in the 34th percentile, on average, in overall leadership effectiveness. But if they had just one outstanding strength, their overall leadership effectiveness score rose to the 64th percentile, on average. In other words, the difference between being in

AN INFORMAL 360

Before you can build on your strengths, you need an objective view of what they are. Ideally, this comes from a formal, confidential 360-degree evaluation. But if that's not possible, a direct approach can work. Try simply asking your team members, colleagues, and boss these simple questions, either in person or in writing.

- What leadership skills do you think are strengths for me?

- Is there anything I do that might be considered a fatal flaw—that could derail my career or lead me to fail in my current job if it's not addressed?

- What leadership ability, if outstanding, would have the most significant impact on the productivity or effectiveness of the organization?

- What leadership abilities of mine have the most significant impact on you?

Do your best to exhibit receptiveness and to create a feeling of safety (especially for direct reports). Make it clear that you're seeking self-improvement. Tell your colleagues explicitly that you are open to negative feedback and that you will absorb it professionally and appropriately—and without retribution. Of course, you need to follow through on this promise, or the entire process will fail.

the bottom third of leaders and being almost in the top third is a single extraordinary strength. Two profound strengths put leaders close to the top quartile, three put them in the top quintile, and four put them nearly in the top decile. (See figure 7-2.)

In this context, a look at Tom's 360 results sheds light on the question of why he was passed over for a plum assignment. Tom had no critical flaws, but he hadn't yet demonstrated any outstanding strengths either.

FIGURE 7-2

What difference can a single strength make?

Raising just one competency to the level of outstanding can up your overall leadership effectiveness ranking from the bottom third to almost the top third.

Percentile Ranking

Leaders with
no outstanding
strengths
34

Leaders with one
64

. . . Two
72

. . . Three
81

. . . Four
89

. . . Five
91

With no strengths above the 70th percentile, he didn't score "good," let alone "outstanding," in overall leadership ability. Anyone in the organization with a single notable strength was likely to outpace him for promotion opportunities. But if Tom could lift just a few of his relative strengths from the 70th to the 80th and then the 90th percentile, his overall leadership effectiveness might go from above average to good to exceptional. Clearly, those strengths merited a closer examination.

Like many people, though, Tom was initially galvanized by the low bars on his chart, which evoked a mixture of guilt and denial. His relatively low score on building relationships called up uncomfortable memories of high school—something he didn't mention as he looked over the results with his boss. But he did say that he couldn't believe he wasn't scored higher on innovativeness, and he started to tick off initiatives he felt he deserved credit for. Maybe he was innovative, and maybe he wasn't. It's common for your self-assessment to vary sharply from everyone else's assessment of you. But remember that it's others' opinions that matter.

When Tom did turn his attention to his strengths, he wasn't surprised to see that he scored well in focusing on results and in solving problems and analyzing issues. Less obvious to him, and perhaps more gratifying, were his relatively high marks in developing strategic perspective and inspiring and motivating others. Now he could move on to the next step.

Choose a strength to focus on

Choices between good and bad are easy. But choices between good and good cause us to deliberate and second-guess. It may not matter which competency Tom selected, since enhancing any one of them would markedly improve his leadership effectiveness. Nevertheless, we recommend that developing leaders focus on a competency that matters to the organization and about which they feel some passion, because a strength you feel passionate about that is not important to your organization is essentially a hobby, and a strength the organization needs that you don't feel passionate about is just a chore.

You can use your colleagues' importance ratings from the 360 assessment to get a somewhat objective view of organizational needs. But the prospect of following his passions alarmed Tom, who didn't know how to begin. Answering a series of questions made the notion more concrete. For each of the 16 competencies, he ran down the following list:

- Do I look for ways to enhance this skill?

- Do I look for new ways to use it?

- Am I energized, not exhausted, when I use it?

- Do I pursue projects in which I can apply this strength?

- Can I imagine devoting time to improving it?

- Would I enjoy getting better at this skill?

Counting his "yes" answers gave Tom a solid way to quantify his passions. A simple worksheet showed him how his skills, his passions, and the organization's needs dovetailed (see figure 7-3). When Tom checked off his

---

FIGURE 7-3

Narrowing down the options

The strength you focus on should be both important to the organization and important to you. A simple worksheet (like Tom's, below) can help you see where your strengths and interests and the needs of your organization converge. Choose five competencies in each of the three categories.

	Your competencies	Your passions	Organizational needs	Total
1. Displays honesty and integrity				
2. Exhibits technical/professional expertise	X			1
3. Solves problems and analyzes issues	X			1
4. Innovates		X	X	2
5. Practices self-development				
6. Focuses on results	X			1
7. Establishes stretch goals				
8. Takes initiative		X		1
9. Communicates powerfully and broadly			X	1
10. Inspires and motivates others	X	X	X	③
11. Builds relationships			X	1
12. Develops others		X		1
13. Collaborates and fosters teamwork		X		1
14. Develops strategic perspective	X		X	2
15. Champions change				
16. Connects the group to the outside world				

top five competencies, his five passions, and the organization's top priorities, he could see a clear convergence. He decided to focus on the strength that, as it happens, we have found to be most universally associated with extraordinary leadership: "inspires and motivates others."

Select a complementary behavior

People who excel at motivating others are good at persuading them to take action and to go the extra mile. They effectively exercise power to influence key decisions for the benefit of the organization. They know how to motivate different people in different ways. So it was not surprising that Tom already did those things pretty well. He scanned the list of competency companions:

- Connects emotionally with others

- Establishes stretch goals

- Exhibits clear vision and direction

- Communicates powerfully and broadly

- Develops others

- Collaborates and fosters teamwork

- Nurtures innovation

- Takes initiative

- Champions change

- Is a strong role model

You should choose a companion behavior that, like a good strength, is important to the organization and makes you feel enthusiastic about tackling it. But at this point it's also constructive to consider your lower scores. In talking these points over with his manager, Tom decided to work on his communication skills, which didn't score particularly high but were high enough that raising them a little could make a significant difference.

Develop it in a linear way

Having settled on a competency companion, Tom could now work at directly improving his basic skills in that area. Strong communicators speak concisely and deliver effective presentations. Their instructions are clear. They write well. They can explain new concepts clearly. They help people understand how their work contributes to broader business objectives. They can translate terms used by people in different functions. Tom saw lots of room for improvement here: No one would ever call him concise; he didn't always finish sentences he'd started; and he found writing a challenge.

We would have recommended that he look for as many opportunities as possible, both inside and outside work, to improve his communication. He could take a course in business writing. He could practice with friends and family, in his church or his community. He could volunteer to make presentations to senior management or ask colleagues to critique some of his memos and emails. He might volunteer to help high school students write college application essays. He could videotape himself making speeches or join a local Toastmasters club.

Tom decided to seek the advice of a colleague whose communication skills he admired. The colleague suggested (among other things) that because writing was not a strong point, Tom should practice communicating more in person or over the phone. This turned out to be challenging: Tom found that before he could even begin, he had to change his approach to email, because he was in the habit of constantly checking and replying to it throughout the day. He couldn't always substitute the phone, because he couldn't make calls while he was in a meeting or talking to someone else. He started to set aside specific times of the day for email so that he could reply by phone or in person—a small change that had unexpected consequences. Instead of being interrupted and distracted at random moments throughout the day (and evening), his staffers had concentrated, direct interactions with him. They found these more efficient and effective, even though they could no longer choose when (or whether) to reply to Tom's cryptic emails. Tom found that he connected better with people he talked to, both because his attention wasn't divided and because he could read their tone of voice and body language. As a result, he absorbed more information, and his colleagues felt he was more attentive to their views.

Tom also started to pay more attention not just to how he was communicating but to what he was saying. His colleague suggested that Tom start to keep track of how often he issued instructions versus how often he asked questions. Tom also took note of how much of what he said was criticism (constructive or otherwise) and how much was encouragement. Increasing the proportion of questions and encouragement had an immediate effect: His team began to understand him more quickly, so he didn't have to repeat himself as often. Several team members actually thanked him for allowing them to express their points of view.

Like Tom, you should expect to see some concrete evidence of improvement within 30 to 60 days. If you don't, what you're doing is not working. That said, complementary behaviors improve steadily with practice, and Tom's progress is typical: Fifteen months later, on taking another 360, he found he'd moved into the 82nd percentile in his ability to inspire. He wasn't extraordinary yet, but he was getting close. Our advice would be to keep at it—to improve another competency companion or two until he reaches the 90th percentile and becomes truly exceptional at inspiring others. Then he can start the entire process again with another strength and its complements, and another—at which point he will be making a uniquely valuable contribution to his company.

Can You Overdo It?

Everyone knows someone who is too assertive, too technically oriented, too focused on driving for results. Many people cite examples like these to argue against the wisdom of improving your leadership effectiveness by strengthening your strengths. Our research does in fact show a point where balance becomes important. The data suggest that the difference between having four profound strengths and having five is a gain of merely 2 percentage points in overall leadership effectiveness. Thus leaders who are already exceptional should consider one more variable.

You will note in figure 7-1 that the 16 differentiating competencies fall into five broader categories: character, personal capability, getting results, interpersonal skills, and leading change. People who have many strengths should consider how they are distributed across those categories and focus improvement efforts on an under-represented one.

But we cannot think of a less constructive approach to improving your leadership effectiveness than treating your strengths as weaknesses. Have you ever known anyone who had too much integrity? Was too effective a communicator? Was just too inspiring? Developing competency companions works precisely because, rather than simply doing more of the same, you are enhancing how you already behave with new ways of working and interacting that will make that behavior more effective.

Focusing on your strengths is hardly a new idea. Forty-four years ago Peter Drucker made the business case eloquently in *The Effective Executive:* "Unless . . . an executive looks for strength and works at making strength productive, he will only get the impact of what a man cannot do, of his lacks, his weaknesses, his impediments to performance and effectiveness. To staff from what there is not and to focus on weakness is wasteful—a misuse, if not abuse, of the human resource." Since then a body of work has grown up supporting and advocating for Drucker's approach. Our own research shows how big a difference developing a few strengths can make. It is distressing to find that fewer than 10% of the executives we work with have any plan to do so.

We are convinced that the problem is less a matter of conviction than of execution. Executives need a path to enhancing their strengths that is as clear as the one to fixing their weaknesses. That is the greatest value, we believe, of the cross-training approach: It allows people to use the linear improvement techniques they know and understand to produce a nonlinear result.

Often executives complain to us that there are not enough good leaders in their organizations. We would argue that in fact far too many leaders are merely good. The challenge is not to replace bad leaders with good ones; it is to turn people like Tom—hardworking, capable executives who are reasonably good at their jobs—into outstanding leaders with distinctive strengths.

John H. Zenger is the CEO, **Joseph R. Folkman** is the president, and **Scott Edinger** is the executive vice president of Zenger Folkman, a leadership development consultancy. They are the authors of *The Inspiring Leader*. Follow Folkman on Twitter @joefolkman. Zenger and Folkman are coauthors of the book *Speed: How Leaders Accelerate Successful Execution*. Edinger is also the founder of Edinger Consulting Group. His latest book is *The Hidden Leader: Discover and Develop Greatness Within Your Company*. Follow him on Twitter @ScottKEdinger.

CHAPTER 8

How to Play to Your Strengths

by Laura Morgan Roberts, Gretchen Spreitzer, Jane Dutton, Robert Quinn, Emily Heaphy, and Brianna Barker Caza

Most feedback accentuates the negative. During formal employee evaluations, discussions invariably focus on "opportunities for improvement," even if the overall evaluation is laudatory. Informally, the sting of criticism lasts longer than the balm of praise. Multiple studies have shown that people pay keen attention to negative information. For example, when asked to recall important emotional events, people remember four negative memories for every positive one. No wonder most

Reprinted from *Harvard Business Review*, January 2005 (product #R0501G).

executives give and receive performance reviews with all the enthusiasm of a child on the way to the dentist.

Traditional, corrective feedback has its place, of course; every organization must filter out failing employees and ensure that everyone performs at an expected level of competence. Unfortunately, feedback that ferrets out flaws can lead otherwise talented managers to overinvest in shoring up or papering over their perceived weaknesses, or forcing themselves onto an ill-fitting template. Ironically, such a focus on problem areas prevents companies from reaping the best performance from its people. After all, it's a rare baseball player who is equally good at every position. Why should a natural third baseman labor to develop his skills as a right fielder?

The alternative, as the Gallup Organization researchers Marcus Buckingham, Donald Clifton, and others have suggested, is to foster excellence in the third baseman by identifying and harnessing his unique strengths. It is a paradox of human psychology that while people remember criticism, they respond to praise. The former makes them defensive and therefore unlikely to change, while the latter produces confidence and the desire to perform better. Managers who build up their strengths can reach their highest potential. This positive approach does not pretend to ignore or deny the problems that traditional feedback mechanisms identify. Rather, it offers a separate and unique feedback experience that counterbalances negative input. It allows managers to tap into strengths they may or may not be aware of and so contribute more to their organizations.

During the past few years, we have developed a powerful tool to help people understand and leverage their individual talents. Called the Reflected Best Self (RBS) exercise, our method allows managers to develop a sense of their "personal best" in order to increase their future potential. The RBS exercise is but one example of new approaches springing from an area of research called positive organizational scholarship (POS). Just as psychologists know that people respond better to praise than to criticism, organizational behavior scholars are finding that when companies focus on positive attributes such as resilience and trust, they can reap impressive bottom-line returns. (For more on this research, see the sidebar "The Positive Organization.") Thousands of executives, as well as tomorrow's leaders enrolled in business schools around the world, have completed the RBS exercise.

In this article, we will walk you through the RBS exercise step-by-step and describe the insights and results it can yield. Before we proceed, however, a few caveats are in order. First, understand that the tool is not designed to stroke your ego; its purpose is to assist you in developing a plan for more effective action. (Without such a plan, you'll keep running in place.) Second, the lessons generated from the RBS exercise can elude you if you don't pay sincere attention to them. If you are too burdened by time pressures and job demands, you may just file the information away and forget about it. To be effective, the exercise requires commitment, diligence, and follow-through. It may even be helpful to have a coach keep you on task. Third, it's important to conduct the RBS exercise at a different time of year than the traditional performance review so that negative feedback from traditional mechanisms doesn't interfere with the results of the exercise.

THE POSITIVE ORGANIZATION

Positive organizational scholarship (POS) is an area of organizational behavior research that focuses on the positive dynamics (such as strength, resilience, vitality, trust, and so on) that lead to positive effects (like improved productivity and performance) in individuals and organizations. The word "positive" refers to the discipline's affirmative bias, "organizational" focuses on the processes and conditions that occur in group contexts, and "scholarship" reflects the rigor, theory, scientific procedures, and precise definition in which the approach is grounded.

The premise of POS research is that by understanding the drivers of positive behavior in the workplace, organizations can rise to new levels of achievement. For example, research by Marcial Losada and Emily Heaphy at the University of Michigan suggests that when individuals or teams hear five positive comments to every negative one, they unleash a level of positive energy that fuels higher levels of individual and group performance. Kim Cameron, a POS researcher, has demonstrated how this positive approach has helped

Used correctly, the RBS exercise can help you tap into unrecognized and unexplored areas of potential. Armed with a constructive, systematic process for gathering and analyzing data about your best self, you can burnish your performance at work.

the workers at Rocky Flats, a nuclear site in Colorado, tackle difficult and dangerous work in record time. Begun in 1995 and estimated to take 70 years and $36 billion, the Rocky Flats cleanup project is now slated for completion in 10 years, with a price tag of less than $7 billion. Kaiser-Hill, the company in charge of the cleanup, replaced a culture of denial with one that fostered employee flexibility and celebrated achievements. The result was that employees developed new procedures that were fast, smart, and safe.

POS does not adopt one particular theory or framework but draws from the full spectrum of organizational theories to explain and predict high performance. To that end, a core part of the POS mission is to create cases, tools, and assessments that can help organizations improve their practices. The Reflected Best Self exercise is just one example of the kinds of practice tools available from POS. (For more information about POS, see the University of Michigan's Web site at www.bus.umich.edu/positive/.)

Step 1: Identify Respondents and Ask for Feedback

The first task in the exercise is to collect feedback from a variety of people inside and outside work. By gathering input from a variety of sources—family members, past and present colleagues, friends, teachers, and so on—you can develop a much broader and richer understanding of yourself than you can from a standard performance evaluation.

As we describe the process of the Reflected Best Self exercise, we will highlight the experience of Robert Duggan (not his real name), whose self-discovery process is typical of the managers we've observed. Having retired from a successful career in the military at a fairly young age and earned an MBA from a top business school, Robert accepted a midlevel management position at an IT services firm. Despite strong credentials and leadership experience, Robert remained stuck in the same position year after year. His performance evaluations were generally good but not strong enough to put him on the high-potential track. Disengaged, frustrated, and disheartened, Robert grew increasingly stressed and disillusioned with his company. His workday felt more and more like an episode of *Survivor*.

Seeking to improve his performance, Robert enrolled in an executive education program and took the RBS exercise. As part of the exercise, Robert gathered feedback from 11 individuals from his past and present who knew him well. He selected a diverse but balanced group—his wife and two other family members, two friends from his MBA program, two colleagues from his time in the army, and four current colleagues.

Robert then asked these individuals to provide information about his strengths, accompanied by specific examples of moments when Robert used those strengths in ways that were meaningful to them, to their families or teams, or to their organizations. Many people—Robert among them—feel uncomfortable asking for exclusively positive feedback, particularly from colleagues. Accustomed to hearing about their strengths and weaknesses simultaneously, many executives imagine any positive feedback will be unrealistic, even false. Some also worry that respondents might construe the request as presumptuous or egotistical. But once managers accept that the exercise will help them improve their performance, they tend to dive in.

Within 10 days, Robert received email responses from all 11 people describing specific instances when he had made important contributions—including pushing for high quality under a tight deadline, being inclusive in communicating with a diverse group, and digging for critical information. The answers he received surprised him. As a military veteran and a technical person holding an MBA, Robert rarely yielded to his emotions. But in reading story after story from his respondents, Robert found himself deeply moved—as if he were listening to appreciative speeches at a party thrown in his honor. The stories were also surprisingly convincing. He had more strengths than he knew. (For more on Step 1, refer to the sidebar "Requesting Feedback.")

Step 2: Recognize Patterns

In this step, Robert searched for common themes among the feedback, adding to the examples with observations of his own, then organizing all the input into a table. (To view parts of Robert's table, see figure 8-1.) Like many who participate in the RBS exercise, Robert expected

REQUESTING FEEDBACK

Here's some sample language to use as you solicit feedback from family, friends, teachers, and colleagues.

Dear Colleague,

I'm currently working on creating a personal development plan. As part of that process, I'm gathering feedback from a variety of people I work with closely to help me develop a broader understanding of the strengths I bring to our work. I'm hoping you'll be willing to share your thoughts with me.

From your perspective, what would you say my professional strengths are? Just two or three would be helpful, and if you could cite a specific example of situations where I used those in ways that were meaningful to you, that would be great. Your candid feedback and examples will help me shape my development plan.

Thank you for taking the time to help me.

Sincerely,

X

---

that, given the diversity of respondents, the comments he received would be inconsistent or even competing. Instead, he was struck by their uniformity. The comments from his wife and family members were similar to those from his army buddies and work colleagues. Everyone took note of Robert's courage under pressure, high ethical standards, perseverance, curiosity, adaptability, re-

FIGURE 8-1

Finding common themes

Creating a table helps you make sense of the feedback you collect. By clustering examples, you can more easily compare resources and identify common themes.

Common theme	Examples given	Possible interpretation
Ethics, values, and courage	• I take a stand when superiors and peers cross the boundaries of ethical behavior. • I am not afraid to stand up for what I believe in. I confront people who litter or who yell at their kids in public.	• I am at my best when I choose the harder right over the easier wrong. I derive even more satisfaction when I am able to teach others. I am professionally courageous.
Curiosity and perseverance	• I gave up my promising career in the military to get my MBA. • I investigated and solved a security breach through an innovative approach.	• I like meeting new challenges. I take risks and persevere despite obstacles.
Ability to build teams	• In high school, I assembled a team of students that helped improve the school's academic standards. • I am flexible and willing to learn from others, and I give credit where credit is due.	• I thrive when working closely with others.

spect for diversity, and team-building skills. Robert suddenly realized that even his small, unconscious behaviors had made a huge impression on others. In many cases, he had forgotten about the specific examples cited until he read the feedback, because his behavior in those situations had felt like second nature to him.

The RBS exercise confirmed Robert's sense of himself, but for those who are unaware of their strengths, the exercise can be truly illuminating. Edward, for example, was a recently minted MBA executive in an automotive firm. His colleagues and subordinates were older and more experienced than he, and he felt uncomfortable disagreeing with them. But he learned through the RBS exercise that his peers appreciated his candid alternative views and respected the diplomatic and respectful manner with which he made his assertions. As a result, Edward grew bolder in making the case for his ideas, knowing that his boss and colleagues listened to him, learned from him, and appreciated what he had to say.

Other times, the RBS exercise sheds a more nuanced light on the skills one takes for granted. Beth, for example, was a lawyer who negotiated on behalf of nonprofit organizations. Throughout her life, Beth had been told she was a good listener, but her exercise respondents noted that the interactive, empathetic, and insightful manner in which she listened made her particularly effective. The specificity of the feedback encouraged Beth to take the lead in future negotiations that required delicate and diplomatic communications.

For naturally analytical people, the analysis portion of the exercise serves both to integrate the feedback and develop a larger picture of their capabilities. Janet, an engineer, thought she could study her feedback as she would a technical drawing of a suspension bridge. She saw her "reflected best self" as something to interrogate and improve. But as she read the remarks from family, friends, and colleagues, she saw herself in a broader and more human context. Over time, the stories she read about her enthusiasm and love of design helped her rethink her career path toward more managerial roles in which she might lead and motivate others.

Step 3: Compose Your Self-Portrait

The next step is to write a description of yourself that summarizes and distills the accumulated information. The description should weave themes from the feedback together with your self-observations into a composite of who you are at your best. The self-portrait is not designed to be a complete psychological and cognitive profile. Rather, it should be an insightful image that you can use as a reminder of your previous contributions and as a guide for future action. The portrait itself should not be a set of bullet points but rather a prose composition beginning with the phrase, "When I am at my best, I . . ." The process of writing out a two- to four-paragraph narrative cements the image of your best self in your consciousness. The narrative form also helps you draw connections between the themes in your life that may previously have seemed disjointed or unrelated. Composing the portrait takes time and demands careful consideration, but at the end of this process, you should come away with a rejuvenated image of who you are.

In developing his self-portrait, Robert drew on the actual words that others used to describe him, rounding out the picture with his own sense of himself at his best. He excised competencies that felt off the mark. This didn't mean he discounted them, but he wanted to assure that the overall portrait felt authentic and powerful. "When I am at my best," Robert wrote,

> *I stand by my values and can get others to understand why doing so is important. I choose the harder right over the easier wrong. I enjoy setting an example. When I am in learning mode and am curious and passionate about a project, I can work intensely and untiringly. I enjoy taking things on that others might be afraid of or see as too difficult. I'm able to set limits and find alternatives when a current approach is not working. I don't always assume that I am right or know best, which engenders respect from others. I try to empower and give credit to others. I am tolerant and open to differences.*

As Robert developed his portrait, he began to understand why he hadn't performed his best at work: He lacked a sense of mission. In the army, he drew satisfaction from the knowledge that the safety of the men and women he led, as well as the nation he served, depended on the quality of his work. He enjoyed the sense of teamwork and variety of problems to be solved. But as an IT manager in charge of routine maintenance on new hardware products, he felt bored and isolated from other people.

The portrait-writing process also helped Robert create a more vivid and elaborate sense of what psychologists would call his "possible self"—not just the person he is in his day-to-day job but the person he might be in completely different contexts. Organizational researchers have shown that when we develop a sense of our best possible self, we are better able make positive changes in our lives.

Step 4: Redesign Your Job

Having pinpointed his strengths, Robert's next step was to redesign his personal job description to build on what he was good at. Given the fact that routine maintenance work left him cold, Robert's challenge was to create a better fit between his work and his best self. Like most RBS participants, Robert found that the strengths the exercise identified could be put into play in his current position. This involved making small changes in the way he worked, in the composition of his team, and in the way he spent his time. (Most jobs have degrees of freedom in all three of these areas; the trick is operating within the fixed constraints of your job to redesign work at the margins, allowing you to better play to your strengths.)

Robert began by scheduling meetings with systems designers and engineers who told him they were having trouble getting timely information flowing between their groups and Robert's maintenance team. If communication improved, Robert believed, new products would not continue to be saddled with the serious and costly maintenance issues seen in the past. Armed with a carefully documented history of those maintenance problems as well as a new understanding of his naturally analytical and creative team-building skills, Robert began meeting regularly with the designers and engineers to brainstorm better ways to prevent problems with new products.

The meetings satisfied two of Robert's deepest best-self needs: He was interacting with more people at work, and he was actively learning about systems design and engineering.

Robert's efforts did not go unnoticed. Key executives remarked on his initiative and his ability to collaborate across functions, as well as on the critical role he played in making new products more reliable. They also saw how he gave credit to others. In less than nine months, Robert's hard work paid off, and he was promoted to program manager. In addition to receiving more pay and higher visibility, Robert enjoyed his work more. His passion was reignited; he felt intensely alive and authentic. Whenever he felt down or lacking in energy, he reread the original email feedback he had received. In difficult situations, the email messages helped him feel more resilient.

Robert was able to leverage his strengths to perform better, but there are cases in which RBS findings conflict with the realities of a person's job. This was true for James, a sales executive who told us he was "in a world of hurt" over his work situation. Unable to meet his ambitious sales goals, tired of flying around the globe to fight fires, his family life on the verge of collapse, James had suffered enough. The RBS exercise revealed that James was at his best when managing people and leading change, but these natural skills did not and could not come into play in his current job. Not long after he did the exercise, he quit his high-stress position and started his own successful company.

Other times, the findings help managers aim for undreamed-of positions in their own organizations. Sarah, a high-level administrator at a university, shared her best-self portrait with key colleagues, asking them to help her identify ways to better exploit her strengths and talents. They suggested that she would be an ideal candidate for a new executive position. Previously, she would never have considered applying for the job, believing herself unqualified. To her surprise, she handily beat out the other candidates.

Beyond Good Enough

We have noted that while people remember criticism, awareness of faults doesn't necessarily translate into better performance. Based on that understanding, the RBS exercise helps you remember your strengths—and construct a plan to build on them. Knowing your strengths also offers you a better understanding of how to deal with your weaknesses—and helps you gain the confidence you need to address them. It allows you to say, "I'm great at leading but lousy at numbers. So rather than teach me remedial math, get me a good finance partner." It also allows you to be clearer in addressing your areas of weakness as a manager. When Tim, a financial services executive, received feedback that he was a great listener and coach, he also became more aware that he had a tendency to spend too much time being a cheerleader and too little time keeping his employees to task. Susan, a senior advertising executive, had the opposite problem: While her feedback lauded her results-oriented management approach, she wanted to be sure that she hadn't missed opportunities to give her employees the space to learn and make mistakes.

In the end, the strength-based orientation of the RBS exercise helps you get past the "good enough" bar. Once you discover who you are at the top of your game, you can use your strengths to better shape the positions you choose to play—both now and in the next phase of your career.

———————

Laura Morgan Roberts is a teaching professor of management at Georgetown University's McDonough School of Business. Her work focuses on cultivating positive identities in diverse work organizations. **Gretchen Spreitzer** is the Keith E. and Valerie J. Alessi Professor of Business Administration at the University of Michigan's Ross School of Business where she is a core faculty member in the Center for Positive Organizations. Her most recent work is looking at positive deviance and how organizations enable employees to thrive. **Jane Dutton** is the Robert L. Kahn Distinguished University Professor Emerita of Business Administration and Psychology at the University of Michigan's Ross School of Business. **Robert Quinn** is a professor emeritus at the University of Michigan's Ross School of Business and a cofounder of the school's Center for Positive Organizations. **Emily Heaphy** is an assistant professor at the University of Massachusetts Amherst. **Brianna Barker Caza** is the Richard Morantz and Sheree Walder Morantz Associate Professor of Business Ethics at the Asper School of Business, University of Manitoba.

CHAPTER 9

Get the Feedback You Need

by Carolyn O'Hara

You need feedback to learn and grow, and if you're waiting for your annual review to find out how you're performing, you're not getting enough of it. But how do you get the focused input you need? And if your boss is stingy with pointers and advice, how do you encourage her to give you more? Who else should you be asking to help you improve?

What the Experts Say

Receiving feedback can be "a stressful experience," says Ed Batista, an executive coach and an instructor at the

Adapted from content posted on hbr.org, May 15, 2015 (product #H022ZB).

Stanford Graduate School of Business. That's why many people hesitate to ask for it. But the more often you do, the less stressful it becomes to initiate the conversation and to hear the comments. "If you're having a feedback conversation every week, there's less to be surprised by and more opportunity to modify your behavior," Batista explains. The process will also make you happier and more productive at work, adds Sheila Heen, author of *Thanks for the Feedback: The Science and Art of Receiving Feedback Well*. "People who go out and solicit negative feedback—meaning they aren't just fishing for compliments—report higher satisfaction," she says. "They adapt more quickly to new roles, get higher performance reviews, and show others they are committed to doing their jobs." Here's how to ask for feedback that helps you get ahead.

Understand What You're Looking For

Think about the kind of feedback you crave. Do you want more appreciation or acknowledgment? Evaluation of your performance on a particular project or task? Or general coaching about how you can improve and learn? Knowing this will help you craft your approach, says Heen. "You can go to your boss and say, 'I feel like I get a ton of appreciation around here. I know I'm valued. What I don't have a sense of is what I need to work on.'" And while advice on areas in which you can develop is often the most useful, "there is value in asking for positive feedback as well," says Batista. Don't hesitate to ask your boss to review your performance on an obviously successful project. "It's can be an opportunity to build a stronger relationship," he says.

Ask for Feedback in Real Time

If you want some insight into how you did on a particular task or how you might improve on the next project, don't dawdle. It's best to ask sooner rather than later. Batista advises that you not try to do it all in one conversation. "Chop it up into manageable chunks and space out the interactions," he says. You also don't have to schedule time in advance or make a formal approach. "Don't think of it as sitting down to have an official conversation," says Heen. "Just reach out to your boss, colleagues, or clients and have a very quick and informal coaching exchange." You might pull your boss aside after a meeting, or close a conversation with a client with a parting request for her reaction to your role on a recent project.

Pose Specific Questions

Whatever you do, don't start off by asking, "Do you have any feedback for me?" "That's a terrible question," says Heen. "The answer is almost always no and you learn nothing." She recommends instead asking, "What's one thing I could improve?" so it's clear that you're asking for coaching and it's clear that you assume there's at least one thing you can work on. You can also tailor the question to the specific situation: "What's one thing I could have done better in that meeting or presentation?" You should also avoid asking questions that are likely to result in yes or no answers. "Asking questions that begin with 'how' or 'what' will elicit fuller responses," Batista says. He suggests questions like, "How did that go from your perspective?" or "What do you think I might have done differently?"

Press for Examples

To get the most out the feedback once you've asked, you may have to probe for specifics. "Sometimes, the person will say, 'I just think you need to be more assertive or more proactive or more of a team player,'" says Heen. "That's vague and what we call a label. It's not very helpful. You have to unpack the label." To do that, ask probing questions like, "Can you explain what you mean?" "How could I have been more assertive just now?" and "What kinds of things should I do to be more assertive going forward?"

Turn to Colleagues

Your boss certainly isn't the only one qualified to give you feedback. "The people in the meeting with you or reading your spreadsheets are the ones who actually have the information to help you improve," Heen says. So when looking for input, don't just look up the organizational chart, but also left, right, and occasionally down. To kickstart a regular feedback loop with colleagues, offer input on, observations about, and praise for their work as well. "You'll get more feedback when you're giving some," says Batista.

On Virtual Teams, Ask More Frequently

It can be particularly hard for virtual team members to get regular feedback since physical distance often prevents informal exchanges. So "the onus is on you" to ask for more input, says Batista. Heen's advice is to "pick up the phone." Don't rely on email because nuances tend to get lost.

Carolyn O'Hara is a writer and editor based in New York City. She's worked at *The Week*, *PBS NewsHour*, and *Foreign Policy*. Follow her on Twitter @carolynohara1.

CHAPTER 10

How Getting Actionable Feedback Can Help You Get Promoted

by Sabina Nawaz

When you rise up through the executive ranks, one of the commodities in scarce supply is actionable feedback from those you report to. An occasional fat bonus or raise fills in the blanks for positive feedback, while being assigned to "special" projects—projects that go nowhere—might signal it's time to move on. What you need to grow is the ability to correct course on the fly. You need consistent, actionable feedback.

Adapted from content posted on hbr.org, October 31, 2017 (product #H03Z0N).

How do you get feedback you can use to become a better leader? Here are five ways to solicit concrete, specific observations that can result in being promoted faster:

- **Be proactive.** Get the feedback you need by asking for it and scheduling a time to receive it. Most people will say yes when asked if they'd be willing to provide feedback, but despite their best intentions, very few follow up. So set a specific time and place to initiate the conversation. For example, carve out time by adding it as an agenda item for a monthly meeting. This frees your manager from the burden of having to remember to follow up and allows them focus on what's most important: their comments. And by initiating the conversation and following through at the appointed time, you're signaling that you're serious about getting their input and improving yourself.

- **Ask questions that require specific answers.** During the conversation, avoid generic assurances by asking questions that elicit specific information. Instead of saying, "Do you have feedback for me?" try something like, "What did you notice at our meeting yesterday when I was framing the topic? What's one thing I did well? What's one thing I should do more of or change?" Avoid questions that can easily yield a yes or no response. Give your boss lots of room to choose how they answer and something concrete to respond to. End with a question such as, "Is there anything else?" At this point in the conversation, you've already warmed up the feedback provider and may receive more valuable insights.

- **Guide your manager to a specific response.** Have you ever asked for and received feedback, only to feel frustrated when you don't know how to implement it? For instance, your manager might tell you, "The one thing I liked the most in our last meeting was that you framed the topic strategically." It's helpful to know that you were viewed as strategic, but it's harder to understand what you need to replicate to be viewed as strategic again by that comment alone. Probe for specific behaviors to better understand what your manager means: "What did I say or do that made my framing strategic?" Now they might say, "You started by making a comparison between the competitive landscape and the customer's problem. Then you tied those takeaways to the corporate strategic pillars. I notice that made the senior vice president sit forward in her seat. Then you revealed a specific challenge we face. The combination of all these elements made you appear strategic." Now you know the steps to replicate next time. Getting down to the behavioral level also enables you to adjust actions that aren't working, so you can avoid cementing bad habits.

- **Dig into compliments.** Your biggest learning opportunity is likely to come from an unexpected area: your strengths. Instead of what you did poorly and need to improve, useful feedback can also be based on what you already do well. How can you make your strength a superpower? For example, a leadership class participant once told me that he found me to be a passionate speaker. I asked, "What do I do or say that conveys passion, and what's the impact on you?" to which he replied, "You speak with your hands a lot and have large gestures. You also vary the tone of your voice quite a bit. The combination keeps me awake and inspires me to pay closer attention." Buoyed by his compliment, I was inspired to further study hand gestures, and started using them more deliberately to land key points when speaking.

- **Listen to criticism—and be gracious.** If your manager does provide you with critical feedback, thank them. If their comments were confusing, paraphrase what you heard and verify that you understood it correctly. Ask short clarifying questions if necessary: "Would you please tell me more about point X?" "At which meeting did you notice this?" "How often have you seen me do this?" "Do you have an example?" Never explain away the feedback. Whether or not you agree with it, this is their perception of how you came across. You don't have to act on all the feedback you receive (in some cases, you might want to look into what someone shares before changing your behavior entirely), but if you want to keep receiving feedback, you have to act in a way that makes others want to give it to you.

To help you move up the promotion ladder, shed light on your blind spots and shine up your strengths. By taking charge of the process, you free up the feedback provider to do only one job: provide you with the input you need to become an outstanding executive.

———————

Sabina Nawaz is a global CEO coach, leadership keynote speaker, and writer working in over 26 countries. She advises C-level executives in *Fortune* 500 corporations, government agencies, nonprofits, and academic organizations. Sabina has spoken at hundreds of seminars, events, and conferences including TEDx and has written for FastCompany.com, Inc.com, and Forbes.com, in addition to hbr.org. Follow her on Twitter @sabinanawaz.

Set Goals for Yourself

CHAPTER 11

Nine Things Successful People Do Differently

by Heidi Grant

Why have you been so successful in reaching some of your goals, but not others? If you aren't sure, you are far from alone in your confusion. It turns out that even brilliant, highly accomplished people are pretty lousy when it comes to understanding why they succeed or fail. The intuitive answer—that you are born predisposed to certain talents and lacking in others—is really just one small piece of the puzzle. In fact, decades of research on achievement suggests that successful people reach their

---

Adapted from content posted on hbr.org, February 25, 2011 (product #H006W2).

goals not simply because of who they are, but more often because of what they do.

1. Get Specific

When you set yourself a goal, try to be as specific as possible. "Lose five pounds" is a better goal than "lose some weight," because it gives you a clear idea of what success looks like. Knowing exactly what you want to achieve keeps you motivated until you get there. Also, think about the specific actions that need to be taken to reach your goal. Just promising you'll "eat less" or "sleep more" is too vague—be clear and precise. "I'll be in bed by 10 p.m. on weeknights" leaves no room for doubt about what you need to do, and whether or not you've actually done it.

2. Seize the Moment to Act On Your Goals

Given how busy most of us are, and how many goals we are juggling at once, it's not surprising that we routinely miss opportunities to act on a goal because we simply fail to notice them. Did you really have no time to work out today? No chance at any point to return that phone call? Achieving your goal means grabbing hold of these opportunities before they slip through your fingers.

To seize the moment, decide when and where you will take each action you want to take, in advance. Again, be as specific as possible (e.g., "If it's Monday, Wednesday, or Friday, I'll work out for 30 minutes before work"). Studies show that this kind of planning will help your brain to detect and seize the opportunity when it arises, increasing your chances of success by roughly 300%.

3. Know Exactly How Far You Have Left to Go

Achieving any goal also requires honest and regular monitoring of your progress—if not by others, then by you, yourself. If you don't know how well you are doing, you can't adjust your behavior or your strategies accordingly. Check your progress frequently—weekly, or even daily, depending on the goal.

4. Be a Realistic Optimist

When you are setting a goal, by all means engage in lots of positive thinking about how likely you are to achieve it. Believing in your ability to succeed is enormously helpful for creating and sustaining your motivation. But whatever you do, don't underestimate how difficult it will be to reach your goal. Most goals worth achieving require time, planning, effort, and persistence. Studies show that thinking things will come to you easily and effortlessly leaves you ill-prepared for the journey ahead, and significantly increases the odds of failure.

5. Focus On Getting Better, Rather Than Being Good

Believing you have the ability to reach your goals is important, but so is believing you can get the ability. Many of us believe that our intelligence, our personality, and our physical aptitudes are fixed—that no matter what we do, we won't improve. As a result, we focus on goals that are all about proving ourselves, rather than developing and acquiring new skills.

Fortunately, decades of research suggest that the belief in fixed ability is completely wrong—abilities of all kinds are profoundly malleable. Embracing the fact that you can change will allow you to make better choices, and reach your fullest potential. People whose goals are about getting better, rather than being good, take difficulty in stride and appreciate the journey as much as the destination.

6. Have Grit

Grit is a willingness to commit to long-term goals and to persist in the face of difficulty. Studies show that gritty people obtain more education in their lifetime and earn higher college GPAs. Grit predicts which cadets will stick out their first grueling year at West Point. In fact, grit even predicts which round contestants will make it to at the Scripps National Spelling Bee.

The good news is, if you aren't particularly gritty now, there is something you can do about it. People who lack grit more often than not believe that they just don't have the innate abilities successful people have. If that describes your own thinking . . . well, there's no way to put this nicely: you are wrong. As I mentioned earlier, effort, planning, persistence, and good strategies are what it really takes to succeed. Embracing this knowledge will not only help you see yourself and your goals more accurately, but also do wonders for your grit.

7. Build Your Willpower Muscle

Your self-control "muscle" is just like the other muscles in your body—when it doesn't get much exercise, it becomes weaker over time. But when you give it regular workouts by putting it to good use, it will grow stronger and stronger, and better able to help you successfully reach your goals.

To build willpower, take on a challenge that requires you to do something you'd honestly rather not do. Give up high-fat snacks, do 100 sit-ups a day, stand up straight when you catch yourself slouching, try to learn a new skill. When you find yourself wanting to give in, give up, or just not bother—don't. Start with just one activity, and make a plan for how you will deal with troubles when they occur ("If I have a craving for a snack, I will eat one piece of fresh or three pieces of dried fruit"). It will be hard in the beginning, but it will get easier, and that's the whole point. As your strength grows, you can take on more challenges and step up your self-control workout.

8. Don't Tempt Fate

No matter how strong your willpower muscle becomes, it's important to always respect the fact that it is limited, and if you overtax it, you will temporarily run out of steam. Don't try to take on two challenging tasks at once, if you can help it (like quitting smoking and dieting at the same time). And don't put yourself in harm's way—many people are overly confident in their ability to resist temptation, and as a result they put themselves in situations where temptations abound. Successful people know not to make reaching a goal harder than it already is.

9. Focus On What You *Will* Do, Not What You *Won't* Do

Do you want to successfully lose weight, quit smoking, or put a lid on your bad temper? Then plan how you will replace bad habits with good ones, rather than focusing only on the bad habits themselves. Research on thought suppression (for example, "Don't think about white bears!") has shown that trying to avoid a thought makes it even more active in your mind. The same holds true when it comes to behavior—by trying not to engage in a bad habit, our habits get strengthened rather than broken.

If you want to change your ways, ask yourself, What will I do instead? For example, if you are trying to gain control of your temper and stop flying off the handle, you might make a plan like "If I am starting to feel angry, then I will take three deep breaths to calm down." By using deep breathing as a replacement for giving in to your anger, your bad habit will get worn away over time until it disappears completely.

It is my hope that, after reading about the nine things successful people do differently, you have gained some insight into all the things you have been doing right all along. Even more important, I hope you are able to identify the mistakes that have derailed you, and use that knowledge to your advantage from now on. Remember, you don't need to become a different person to become a more successful one. It's never what you are, but what you do.

Heidi Grant, PhD, is a social psychologist who researches, writes, and speaks about the science of motivation. She is global director of research and development at the NeuroLeadership Institute and serves as associate director of Columbia University's Motivation Science Center. She received her doctorate in social psychology from Columbia University. Her most recent book is *Reinforcements: How to Get People to Help You* (Harvard Business Review Press, 2018). She's also the author of *Nine Things Successful People Do Differently* (Harvard Business Review Press, 2012) and *No One Understands You and What to Do About It* (Harvard Business Review Press, 2015).

CHAPTER 12

Stop Setting Goals You Don't Actually Care About

by Elizabeth Grace Saunders

One January, I asked myself a question: "How can I make achieving my professional growth goals effortless?" I found the answer was elegantly simple—by focusing on alignment goals.

Many people fail on their professional development goals for the year because they take on a lot of goals—goals that they feel they "should" do but ultimately don't energize them. For example, maybe they tell themselves that they need to read a pile of books in order to learn

---

Adapted from content posted on hbr.org, December 30, 2016 (product #H03DCN).

more, keep up with their colleagues, or just stay up-to-date with their industry. But if sitting down to read feels more like a chore, it's unlikely they'll make any progress—and they may feel badly for not achieving their goal when the year comes to a close. While the goal itself may feel as if it is something that fits the needs of their professional role, it doesn't match the individual's preferences or ambitions.

Pick Your Goals

If you want to succeed with your professional growth goals, choose one or two key areas of focus that align with what really matters to you.

For example, this year, I decided to make writing a book proposal for a new book my primary professional development goal. I knew this was the right direction because I felt a lasting surge of energy behind the idea. It had been on my mind since the fall, and I couldn't wait to get started that January.

Nothing about writing the proposal felt like a "should." It felt like a "must." I was excited to move ahead and willing to cut back in other areas of my business to make room for this to happen. This congruence between my internal desires and my external goal made moving ahead relatively effortless.

To begin thinking of your own professional development goals, start by asking yourself three questions:

- If I could accomplish just one major professional development goal this year, what would it be?

- When I think about working on this goal, do I get excited about the process as well as the outcome?

- Is my motivation to pursue this goal intrinsic, something coming from within because it is personally interesting and important, or is it extrinsic, something that I feel would please other people?

These three questions will help you identify what really motivates you internally. Also, I'd recommend keeping the number of goals you choose as narrow as possible, so you can give them your full attention.

Make Time in Your Schedule

Selecting *what* you want to work on can often feel easier than actually moving toward those goals, especially when you're faced with other work commitments. In order to reach these objectives, you need to ensure you've aligned your time with them as well. An integral part of the process of setting a goal is creating time to achieve that goal.

I've always been a huge fan of time blocking as a way to reserve time for important items. But in the past, time for professional development goals was usually slotted in around other work responsibilities, like coaching calls with my time management clients. Even when I was writing my first two books, I would block out half days, at most, to get the writing done. Doing so gave me focused time to concentrate, but it also meant that I ended up working longer hours when I was working on special projects.

This year, though, I decided that I wanted to align my time more firmly with my priorities. That meant blocking out an entire day once a week (I chose Wednesdays) to focus on my book proposal and, once that was sold, my book writing. But rather than simply marking it down, I took it a step further: I put up an out-of-office for each Tuesday and Wednesday to let people know I was out for book writing on Wednesday, and would respond to Tuesday and Wednesday emails on Thursday.

At first, this felt uncomfortable, and I worried about getting everything done. But after making this a lifestyle since the beginning of the year, I realized that it was not only possible, but it felt amazing. I overcame my limiting belief that when I worked on big projects, I had to work longer hours.

Once you decide on your professional development goal or goals for the year, I encourage you to take a similar approach to aligning your time with your goals to make the results effortless. Most people can't block out an entire day every week, but almost everyone can start to reserve more time for their professional development goals than they do now. It may take some time for your colleagues to adjust to the fact that you're not always available. But typically, you can make a consistent investment in your own growth.

To do so, decide on which days and times you can commit to moving ahead on your goal. You may have the opportunity to do something like I did, where you block out an entire day (maybe to take a training class), or you may need to set aside smaller chunks of time. For example, some of my time-coaching clients will set aside two to three hours on a Wednesday morning, come into the office early a couple of days a week, or pick a weeknight or a weekend morning where they can spend an hour moving ahead on their goal. Try one strategy and see how it works. If it seems to suit you and your colleagues, stick with it. If not, adjust the days or times until you get something that fits.

If you plan on working on professional development during the day, you may need to discuss with your boss what's appropriate before making these changes. I also recommend shutting your door, going to a conference room, or working from home. The physical boundary is a great help to avoid the time getting derailed by drive-by meetings.

The exact amount of time you can spend will vary depending on your other responsibilities. But it's important that you're consistently setting aside the time for your professional development goals. It may feel uncomfortable at first, but in time it will get more natural. This will create alignment between what you say matters to you and where you invest your time.

When you have professional development goals that reflect what's important to you and you align your time with those goals, you'll find the results can feel effortless in the year ahead.

Elizabeth Grace Saunders is a time management coach and the founder of Real Life E Time Coaching &

Speaking. She is author of *How to Invest Your Time Like Money* (Harvard Business Review Press, 2015) and *Divine Time Management* (FaithWords, 2017). Find out more at www.RealLifeE.com.

CHAPTER 13

Before You Set New Goals, Think About What You're Going to Stop Doing

by Elizabeth Grace Saunders

What keeps most of us from accomplishing resolutions we set? The pervasive trap of not consciously taking old activities out of our schedule to make room for the new. It's the equivalent of trying to stuff more papers into a file drawer that's already packed tight or going into debt

---

Adapted from content posted on hbr.org, February 5, 2018 (product #H044WF).

to cover additional purchases. You can take the pinch for a little while, but soon you're stretched too thin and need to recalibrate to get back to a sustainable lifestyle (or filing system).

Pausing to consider what needs to be removed from your schedule takes time. But it makes all the difference between being busy and being effective. Here are a few practices that can help you streamline your schedule and build in room to complete your new goals and resolutions.

Question *All* of Your Work Commitments

In many work environments, tasks and projects get piled on without any clear sense of priorities or time capacity. Take time to clean house and reevaluate what you're doing and how you're doing it.

Start by reviewing your current projects and asking yourself a few questions: Does completing this project still make sense? Am I the correct person to work on this project? Would it be more realistic to move this project to a different quarter? Depending on your position, you may or may not have the ability to make unilateral decisions. But if you've taken the time to step back and consider the big picture, you at least have the opportunity to discuss the possibilities with your boss and your team. One of the fastest ways to complete a project is to decide it's not getting done.

If you're struggling with evaluating your work commitments, it may be helpful to chart your professional commitments. For instance, in my book *The 3 Secrets to*

Effective Time Investment, I recommend a chart that includes columns for activity name, type (that is, constant or varied), hours/month, professional importance, personal satisfaction, optional, and length of term. Create a similar chart with column headings tailored to your situation to evaluate your personal commitments. Then use this data to determine what is the highest value to hold on to and what's best let go.

Once you've determined what you might want to carve out of your schedule, begin to make the shifts in what you're doing. It may take time to get buy-in to eliminate, delay, or delegate projects, but over the course of a few weeks or months, your schedule will begin to open up.

Reassess Your Work Style

After addressing the "what," turn your attention toward "how" you accomplish work. Reducing meetings can be a powerful force to create space for focused work. Question whether you need meetings for certain projects as well as their length and frequency. For example, going from a weekly 60-minute meeting to a biweekly 45-minute meeting can save each meeting attendee 2.5 hours a month. Multiply that over multiple meetings, and you could get days of your workweek back.

On the other hand, if you find yourself interrupted throughout the day by drive-by questions, consider setting office hours or standing one-on-one sessions where you make yourself intentionally available. Then define other times when you shut your door—or as one of my time management coaching clients found to be effective, have it mostly shut. It signals to people to not come in unless it's truly urgent. This lessens the time you spend dealing with interruptions and transitioning back to the task at hand.

Finally, consider if there are ways that you can interact less with messaging technology. Decreasing the amount of time spent on email, social media, or other communication channels can dramatically increase the amount of time you have to get work done as well as the speed at which you can complete it. I've found it helpful to limit the amount of time I spend on email each day. I also check social media notifications about once a day, strictly limit notifications to my phone, and purposely avoid adopting every new technology. When you're not on something, you don't need to check it.

Add New Goals Strategically

Once you intentionally create space, you can strategically add in the activities that you want in your life. Sometimes that means simply having the ability to take a break during the day and not work at a frenetic pace. It could mean moving ahead on an important project you've neglected for months. Or it may give you the ability to reduce your hours, so instead of working the second shift at night, you're hitting the gym or spending time with family or friends.

To say yes to the new, you must say no to some of the old. By eliminating some of the activities in your calendar that are no longer the best use of your time, you can finally make progress on what's truly important to you.

Elizabeth Grace Saunders is a time management coach and the founder of Real Life E Time Coaching & Speaking. She is author of *How to Invest Your Time Like Money* (Harvard Business Review Press, 2015) and *Divine Time Management* (FaithWords, 2017). Find out more at www.RealLifeE.com.

Become a Better Learner

CHAPTER 14

Learning to Learn

by Erika Andersen

Organizations today are in constant flux. Industries are consolidating, new business models are emerging, new technologies are being developed, and consumer behaviors are evolving. For executives, the ever-increasing pace of change can be especially demanding. It forces them to understand and quickly respond to big shifts in the way companies operate and how work must get done. In the words of Arie de Geus, a business theorist, "The ability to learn faster than your competitors may be the only sustainable competitive advantage."

I'm not talking about relaxed armchair or even structured classroom learning. I'm talking about resisting the bias against doing new things, scanning the horizon for

Reprinted from *Harvard Business Review*, March 2016 (product #R1603J).

growth opportunities, and pushing yourself to acquire radically different capabilities—while still performing your job. That requires a willingness to experiment and become a novice again and again: an extremely discomforting notion for most of us.

Over decades of coaching and consulting to thousands of executives in a variety of industries, however, my colleagues and I have come across people who succeed at this kind of learning. We've identified four attributes they have in spades: aspiration, self-awareness, curiosity, and vulnerability. They truly want to understand and master new skills; they see themselves very clearly; they constantly think of and ask good questions; and they tolerate their own mistakes as they move up the learning curve.

Of course, these things come more naturally to some people than to others. But, drawing on research in psychology and management as well as our work with clients, we have identified some fairly simple mental tools anyone can develop to boost all four attributes—even those that are often considered fixed (aspiration, curiosity, and vulnerability).

Aspiration

It's easy to see aspiration as either there or not: You want to learn a new skill or you don't; you have ambition and motivation or you lack them. But great learners can raise their aspiration level—and that's key, because everyone is guilty of sometimes resisting development that is critical to success.

Think about the last time your company adopted a new approach—overhauled a reporting system, replaced a CRM platform, revamped the supply chain. Were you eager to go along? I doubt it. Your initial response was probably to justify not learning. (*It will take too long. The old way works just fine for me. I bet it's just a flash in the pan.*) When confronted with new learning, this is often our first roadblock: We focus on the negative and unconsciously reinforce our lack of aspiration.

When we *do* want to learn something, we focus on the positive—what we'll gain from learning it—and envision a happy future in which we're reaping those rewards. That propels us into action. Researchers have found that shifting your focus from challenges to benefits is a good way to increase your aspiration to do initially unappealing things. For example, when Nicole Detling, a psychologist at the University of Utah, encouraged aerialists and speed skaters to picture themselves benefiting from a particular skill, they were much more motivated to practice it.

A few years ago I coached a CMO who was hesitant to learn about big data. Even though most of his peers were becoming converts, he'd convinced himself that he didn't have the time to get into it and that it wouldn't be that important to his industry. I finally realized that this was an aspiration problem and encouraged him to think of ways that getting up to speed on data-driven marketing could help him personally. He acknowledged that it would be useful to know more about how various segments of his customer base were responding to his team's online advertising and in-store marketing campaigns. I then invited him to imagine the situation he'd be in a year later if he was getting that data. He started to show some excitement, saying, "We would be testing different approaches simultaneously, both in-store and online; we'd have good, solid information about which ones were working and for whom; and we could save a lot of time and money by jettisoning the less effective approaches faster." I could almost feel his aspiration rising. Within a few months he'd hired a data analytics expert, made a point of learning from her on a daily basis, and begun to rethink key campaigns in light of his new perspective and skills.

Self-Awareness

Over the past decade or so, most leaders have grown familiar with the concept of self-awareness. They understand that they need to solicit feedback and recognize how others see them. But when it comes to the need for learning, our assessments of ourselves—what we know and don't know, skills we have and don't have—can still be woefully inaccurate. In one study conducted by David Dunning, a Cornell University psychologist, 94% of college professors reported that they were doing "above average work." Clearly, almost half were wrong—many extremely so—and their self-deception surely diminished any appetite for development. Only 6% of respondents saw themselves as having a lot to learn about being an effective teacher.

In my work I've found that the people who evaluate themselves most accurately start the process inside their own heads: They accept that their perspective is often biased or flawed and then strive for greater objectivity, which leaves them much more open to hearing and acting on others' opinions. The trick is to pay attention to how you talk to yourself about yourself and then question the validity of that "self-talk."

Let's say your boss has told you that your team isn't strong enough and that you need to get better at assessing and developing talent. Your initial reaction might be something like *What? She's wrong. My team is strong.* Most of us respond defensively to that sort of criticism. But as soon as you recognize what you're thinking, ask yourself, *Is that accurate? What facts do I have to support it?* In the process of reflection you may discover that you're wrong and your boss is right, or that the truth lies somewhere in between—you cover for some of your reports by doing things yourself, and one of them is inconsistent in meeting deadlines; however, two others are stars. Your inner voice is most useful when it reports the facts of a situation in this balanced way. It should serve as a "fair witness" so that you're open to seeing the areas in which you could improve and how to do so.

One CEO I know was convinced that he was a great manager and leader. He did have tremendous industry knowledge and great instincts about growing his business, and his board acknowledged those strengths. But he listened only to people who affirmed his view of himself and dismissed input about shortcomings; his team didn't feel engaged or inspired. When he finally started to question his assumptions (*Is everyone on my team focused and productive? If not, is there something I could be doing differently?*), he became much more aware of his developmental needs and open to feedback. He realized that it wasn't enough to have strategic insights; he had to share them with his reports and invite discussion, and then set clear priorities—backed by quarterly team and individual goals, regular progress checks, and troubleshooting sessions.

Curiosity

Kids are relentless in their urge to learn and master. As John Medina writes in *Brain Rules,* "This need for explanation is so powerfully stitched into their experience that some scientists describe it as a drive, just as hunger and thirst and sex are drives." Curiosity is what makes us try something until we can do it, or think about something until we understand it. Great learners retain this childhood drive, or regain it through another application of self-talk. Instead of focusing on and reinforcing initial disinterest in a new subject, they learn to ask themselves "curious questions" about it and follow those questions up with actions. Carol Sansone, a psychology researcher, has found, for example, that people can increase their willingness to tackle necessary tasks by thinking about how they could do the work differently to make it more interesting. In other words, they change their self-talk from *This is boring* to *I wonder if I could . . . ?*

You can employ the same strategy in your working life by noticing the language you use in thinking about things that already interest you—*How . . . ? Why . . . ? I wonder . . . ?*—and drawing on it when you need to become curious. Then take just one step to answer a question you've asked yourself: Read an article, query an expert, find a teacher, join a group—whatever feels easiest.

I recently worked with a corporate lawyer whose firm had offered her a bigger job that required knowledge of employment law—an area she regarded as "the single most boring aspect of the legal profession." Rather than trying to persuade her otherwise, I asked her what she was curious about and why. "Swing dancing," she said. "I'm fascinated by the history of it. I wonder how it developed, and whether it was a response to the Depression—it's such a happy art form. I watch great dancers and think about why they do certain things." (See figure 14-1.)

FIGURE 14-1

Changing your inner narrative

I don't need to learn this.	What would my future look like if I did?
I'm already fine at this.	Am I really? How do I compare with my peers?
This is boring.	I wonder why others find it interesting.
I'm terrible at this.	I'm making beginner mistakes but I'll get better.

I explained that her "curious language" could be applied to employment law. "I wonder how anyone could find it interesting?" she said jokingly. I told her that was actually an OK place to start. She began thinking out loud about possible answers ("Maybe some lawyers see it as a way to protect both their employees and their companies . . . ") and then proposed a few other curious questions ("How might knowing more about this make me a better lawyer?").

Soon she was intrigued enough to connect with a colleague who was experienced in employment law. She asked him what he found interesting about it and how he had acquired his knowledge, and his answers prompted other questions. Over the following months she learned what she needed to know for that aspect of her new role.

The next time you're asked to learn something at the office, or sense that you should because colleagues are doing so, encourage yourself to ask and answer a few curious questions about it—*Why are others so excited about this? How might this make my job easier?*—and then seek out the answers. You'll need to find just one thing about a "boring" topic that sparks your curiosity.

Vulnerability

Once we become good or even excellent at some things, we rarely want to go back to being *not* good at other things. Yes, we're now taught to embrace experimentation and "fast failure" at work. But we're also taught to play to our strengths. So the idea of being bad at something for weeks or months; feeling awkward and slow; having to ask "dumb," "I-don't-know-what-you're-talking-about" questions; and needing step-by-step guidance again and again is extremely scary. Great learners allow themselves to be vulnerable enough to accept that beginner state. In fact, they become reasonably comfortable in it—by managing their self-talk.

Generally, when we're trying something new and doing badly at it, we think terrible thoughts: *I hate this. I'm such an idiot. I'll never get this right. This is so frustrating!* That static in our brains leaves little bandwidth for learning. The ideal mindset for a beginner is both vulnerable and balanced: *I'm going to be bad at this to start with, because I've never done it before. AND I know I can learn to do it over time.* In fact, the researchers Robert Wood and Albert Bandura found in the late 1980s that when people are encouraged to expect mistakes and learn from them early in the process of acquiring new skills, the result is "heightened interest, persistence, and better performance."

I know a senior sales manager from the United States who was recently tapped to run the Asia-Pacific region for his company. He was having a hard time acclimating to living overseas and working with colleagues from other cultures, and he responded by leaning on his sales expertise rather than acknowledging his beginner status in the new environment. I helped him recognize his resistance to being a cultural novice, and he was able to shift his self-talk from *This is so uncomfortable—I'll just focus on what I already know* to *I have a lot to learn about Asian cultures. I'm a quick study, so I'll be able to pick it up.* He told me it was an immediate relief: Simply acknowledging his novice status made him feel less foolish and more relaxed. He started asking the necessary questions, and soon he was seen as open, interested, and beginning to understand his new environment.

The ability to acquire new skills and knowledge quickly and continually is crucial to success in a world of rapid change. If you don't currently have the aspiration, self-awareness, curiosity, and vulnerability to be an effective learner, these simple tools can help you get there.

————————

Erika Andersen is the founding partner of Proteus International and the author of *Growing Great Employees*, *Being Strategic*, *Leading So People Will Follow*, and *Be Bad First*.

CHAPTER 15

Four Ways to Become a Better Learner

by Monique Valcour

The CEO sitting across from me is explaining how he and the other executives of a telecommunications firm were caught off guard by a new technology that disrupted the firm's business. "We did not see WhatsApp coming," he says, shaking his head. He wants to increase his capacity to learn, to spot and understand developments inside and outside of the firm. He believes this is vital not only for better performance now, but also for the continued success of his career. "I'm in my early 50s, and I'm afraid

Adapted from content posted on hbr.org, December 31, 2015 (product #H02L4C).

that the next time I want to change jobs, people will see me as irrelevant. I've seen it happen to plenty of others. How do I stay fresh and convince people that I still have a lot to contribute?"

His hunch is right on target. Research shows that leaders who think and act from the same assumptions and behavioral repertoires they've used for years are prone to stagnate, underperform, or derail. As David Peterson, director of executive coaching and leadership at Google, puts it, "Staying within your comfort zone is a good way to prepare for today, but it's a terrible way to prepare for tomorrow." To sustain success, you must develop learning agility.

What Is Learning Agility?

Learning agility is the capacity for rapid, continuous learning from experience. Agile learners are good at making connections across experiences, and they're able to let go of perspectives or approaches that are no longer useful—in other words, they can unlearn things when novel solutions are required. People with this mindset tend to be oriented toward learning goals and open to new experiences. They experiment, seek feedback, and reflect systematically.

A desire to develop by acquiring new skills and mastering new situations is a fundamental element of learning agility. Agile learners value and derive satisfaction from the process of learning itself, which boosts their motivation as well as their capacity to learn from challenging developmental experiences.

As a result, they don't get defensive and they're willing to take risks, such as making a mistake or appearing nonexpert in public. The CEO in the opening paragraph epitomizes nondefensiveness. Our conversation took place at the Institute of Coaching (a Harvard Medical School affiliate) Leadership Forum, held at IESE Business School. He talked openly about his challenges and fears, inviting feedback from four executive coaches whom he'd just met. Unfortunately, many leaders miss out on key learning opportunities because they avoid questioning themselves or intentionally moving outside of their comfort zone.

Learning agility also involves being open to new experiences, people, and information. Two senior management professors I've encountered at academic conferences over the years exemplify opposite ends of the spectrum. Professor A has a voracious appetite for new ideas. Despite his lofty academic stature, he converses just as enthusiastically with graduate students and junior faculty from little-known universities as he does with fellow academic stars, and he collaborates with a wide variety of scholars. Well into his 70s, he's vibrant, energetic, and recognized as an active leader in his research domain. Professor B, by contrast, shows little interest in scholars outside of his familiar circle of followers. His presentations generally rehash old ideas; it's been a long time since he produced anything new. Although he made many important contributions earlier in his career, the low level of learning agility he exhibits now accompanies his fading reputation. He's fallen into the exact career trap the CEO is seeking to avoid.

How Do You Develop Learning Agility?

Since developing learning agility involves learning to recognize and change automatic routines, the aid of a coach can be invaluable. Coaching, which Peterson calls "the ultimate customized learning solution," helps clients understand how their minds work and how to make them work better. But even if you're not working with a coach, there are steps you can take on your own to enhance your learning agility.

Ask for feedback

Think of one or more people who interacted with you or observed your performance on a given task. Tell them you'd value their perspective on how you did, and ask what you could do differently the next time. To maximize learning from their feedback—and this is vital—restrain any urge to defend yourself. Thank them for their input, and then ask yourself what you can learn.

To reduce your defensiveness and develop a learning mindset, consider adopting a motto like Peterson's: "There has to be a better way, and I don't know it yet." The power of the motto lies in the word "yet." As research on growth mindset by psychologist Carol Dweck has found, if you hold the view that there is always more to learn and embrace the process of wading into unfamiliar waters, you can free your thinking, dissolve your fear of failure, and power your success.

Experiment with new approaches or behaviors

To identify new behaviors for testing, Peterson recommends reflecting on a challenge you're facing and asking yourself questions such as "What's one thing I could do to change the outcome of the situation?" and "What will I do differently in the future?" You can also conduct thought experiments, unearthing possibilities from trying out a different point of view. For example, one of my clients was concerned about leading the first team development offsite with her new team of highly talented country managers. With some reflection, she realized that she had gotten stuck in the perspective that in order to be seen as credible, she had to know more than they did. Since she was new, this was impossible. Holding on to that perspective would have caused her stress and undermined her credibility. By letting go of the assumption that she had to be the subject-matter expert and adopting the perspective that she could add greater value as a facilitator, she was able to design and conduct a meeting at which creative ideas flowed freely. The team, which had previously suffered from poor coordination, developed more collaborative relationships.

Look for connections across seemingly unrelated areas

For example, Peterson has systematically applied principles he's used to learn about wine to the domain of leadership development. Oenologists develop expertise by trying many different wines, comparing them, and discussing them with fellow experts. Borrowing these principles, Peterson realized that he could extend his mastery of leadership development by seeking out a wide variety of leaders to coach, comparing leaders to each other on various qualities, and discussing leaders with other experts. To try this technique yourself, choose a domain you have expertise in but that's unrelated to your work and ask yourself how you might apply that knowledge to your current challenge.

Make time for reflection

A growing body of research shows that systematically reflecting on work experiences boosts learning significantly. To ensure continuous progress, get into the habit of asking yourself questions like "What have I learned from this experience?" and "What turned out differently than I expected?" Leaders who demonstrate and encourage reflection not only learn more themselves, but also spur increased contextual awareness and reflective practice in others, thereby laying a foundation for higher levels of learning agility in their teams and organizations.

Practicing these strategies will help you extract the maximum learning from experience. What did our CEO learn? Among other things, he realized that he's been seeking advice on a current challenge from people in his network who are likely to have similar perspectives, and that he stands to learn a great deal from two individuals in different industries. He articulated what he hoped to learn from talking with them and scheduled a time to pick up the phone the next morning.

Monique Valcour is an executive coach, keynote speaker, and management professor. She helps clients create and sustain fulfilling and high-performance jobs, careers, workplaces, and lives. Follow her on Twitter @moniquevalcour.

CHAPTER 16

You Can Learn and Get Work Done at the Same Time

by Liane Davey

As you think about how you want to learn and grow, you don't need to build your development plan around a formal learning program. Although we default to equating development with structured, instructor-led activities, you'd be better served to think of formal programs as the appetizer or dessert of your development, rather than the main course.

You take three risks when you depend on formal courses for nourishment. First, you risk being disappointed if your request can't be funded because other

Adapted from content posted on hbr.org, January 11, 2016 (product #H02LPH).

priorities take precedent. Second, you underestimate how costly it is for you to be away from work, both in your increased workload before and after the training and in the price your team pays in backfilling for you. Finally, focusing on formal development can reinforce a passive mindset and leave you with the false impression that your development is in someone else's hands.

You can fulfill the majority of your development needs on the job. By "on the job," I mean taking activities that you would be completing anyway and using them to develop a new skill. Once you have this sort of development mindset, a team meeting can become a chance to strengthen your communication skills. A morning of returning email can become an opportunity to apply a new organization system. An afternoon of customer interactions can become a chance to hone your business development pitch.

The following practices can help you integrate learning into your workload.

Pick a skill you want to develop

Identify a skill that's valued in your organization. Someone in human resources can tell you if your company has a competency model or career ladder, which describes the most important knowledge, skills, and attributes for a given career path. In the absence of an official list of competencies, ask for ideas from your manager or your colleagues about the skills that would be most vital for you to develop. I highly recommend choosing only one—make it a meaty one—and then using it as a theme that will carry you through the year. Some examples might include becoming a more strategic thinker, improving communication skills, or enhancing your presence and personal brand.

Research the skill you're trying to develop

You can find blogs from subject-matter experts on almost any topic, not to mention a nearly infinite supply of YouTube videos. All told, you have a lifetime of learning at your fingertips. Find spare moments to read up on the skill and keep a folder where you can begin to classify the skill into different subcomponents. For example, if you're working to improve your communication skills, your research might reveal that communication can be broken down into sharpening your ideas and content, clarifying your writing, enhancing your oral communication skills, and improving your listening skills. Whether you want to use old-school index cards or a high-tech app, organize and track what you learn in a way that allows you to drill down several layers into each component. You'll find that once you zero in on one component, new distinctions will be revealed. For example, oral communication will require that you improve both your verbal and nonverbal presentation.

Set a series of progressive goals

Once you understand the different components of the skill you're building, choose one and break it down even further. In the communication example, you might decide that the content of your ideas is strong but you struggle to express your ideas in a meeting because you're quiet. Start by setting your end goal and then work backward to create a series of small but meaningful steps. If you aspire to participate more actively and to have your ideas heard and appreciated by your teammates, start by committing to make one comment in your next team meeting. Once you've practiced being more vocal, your goals can evolve to making your points more concisely or getting comfortable disagreeing with someone in a public forum. Create a cheat sheet for yourself with these goals in order and check them off as you accomplish them.

Ask a colleague for feedback

You'll accelerate your progress when you ask a colleague how you're doing. Tell the person what you're working on to start the conversation and get some generic feedback or advice from them. Then share your specific goals and ask the person to watch and provide feedback on those goals. Don't make this formal or cumbersome, just a quick check-in. In the communication example, as you're walking into the team meeting, say, "I'm working on being more concise. Can you pay attention and let me know how I do?" Then as you're walking out of the meeting, you can get immediate feedback and a few pointers. Occasionally have a lengthier discussion about what your colleague is observing and what he would recommend you work on next.

Once you've achieved one goal, move on to the next. Work through all the goals until you've mastered one component of the skill. Then move on to the next component and repeat the same process. With a skill such as communication, you can devote an entire year (and likely an entire lifetime) to exploring and refining your skills. Refer to your efforts in your performance management conversations so your manager understands what you're working on and can support you.

When you use the activities you're already engaged in as the forum for building new skills, you take control of your own development. You aren't overwhelmed by adding tasks to your already overflowing calendar. You aren't losing accountability by abdicating the responsibility for your growth and development. You're nourishing yourself with a steady diet of learning.

And then you're entitled to a little dessert. Once you've learned what you can from free resources, applied new concepts and built new skills, and done the difficult work of seeking out and acting on feedback, you've earned access to a formal learning program and you shouldn't be sheepish about asking for it. With the investment you've already made, you'll be in a great position to benefit from what you learn.

Liane Davey is the cofounder of 3COze Inc. She is the author of *You First: Inspire Your Team to Grow Up, Get Along, and Get Stuff Done* and a coauthor of *Leadership Solutions: The Pathway to Bridge the Leadership Gap.* Follow her on Twitter@LianeDavey.

CHAPTER 17

Four Practices of People Who Are Always Learning New Skills

by Mike Kehoe

Working in online learning, I've found that every January there's a burst of sign-ups from workers seeking new skills. Perhaps it's a matter of New Year's resolutions, or a reaction to seeing their friends and colleagues make big career changes at this time.

Unfortunately, the initial commitment to learning all too often fizzles. Studies have found that 40% to 80% of

---

Adapted from content posted on hbr.org, January 31, 2018 (product #H044PF).

students drop out of online classes. Those who give up miss out. In one survey of more than 50,000 learners who completed MOOCs on Coursera, 72% reported career benefits such as doing their current job more effectively, finding a new job, or receiving a raise.

Having worked in human resources at a large banking corporation and in strategic HR consulting, I've seen the effects of learning and development on career mobility—and what leads people to let it fall by the wayside. I've found that four crucial practices can make a tremendous difference.

Focus on emerging skills

Job requirements are quickly evolving. To ensure relevance, focus on learning the latest skills. You can do this in a couple of ways.

First, track what skills the leaders in your industry are hiring for. Look at recent job postings from the top companies, and see which qualifications keep popping up. Second, reach out to people in your network or on LinkedIn who have the job you want. If you'd like to know what sales skills and technologies are becoming most important, talk to some high-level salespeople. Ask them what they're learning to keep succeeding at their work and what skills they think someone needs to acquire in order to become a viable candidate.

You may feel intimidated about reaching out to your network. But most of the time, people are happy to share this information. They want to see more and more capable candidates filling jobs and staying on top of trends.

As you get a sense of the most important skills to learn, ask these experts whether they can recommend specific online courses with practical value. Also take a close look at course descriptions to find content that will be useful on the job rather than provide mostly academic insight. For instance, you might seek out instructors who are leading experts in your industry or content created in conjunction with companies that you admire.

Get synchronous

Micro-learning—engaging with online learning tools when and where it's convenient—is becoming a much larger part of the training and development scene. This has its benefits, including freedom, convenience, and digestible content.

But there's also a downside. These asynchronous experiences are often solitary. And without at least some real-time interaction, whether in person or online, many students lose motivation. Research by Joanne M. McInnerney and Tim S. Roberts has found that "the sense of isolation" for some online learners "may make the difference between a successful and an unsuccessful online learning environment." They call for more *synchronous* experiences. Ricardo Mendoza-Gonzalez has also identified interaction and collaboration as critical factors in fruitful learning.

In my work, I've consistently seen that when online students sign up for a live course, in which they interact with a professor and one another at a set time at least once a week, they stick with it longer and learn more.

Often, these kinds of programs offer materials you can work on individually. But the camaraderie can serve as a huge motivator, as can the desire not to fall behind the group.

When a live course isn't available, find a "synchronous cohort"—a friend or acquaintance with similar learning goals. Make a pact to do online learning together weekly. You can learn a lot from hearing each other's questions and explaining things to each other as you come to understand them, since the act of teaching can improve content understanding, recall, and application.

Implement learning immediately

Research by Christopher R. Madan and Anthony Singhal shows that performing the tasks you've learned is crucial, because "enactment enhances memory by serving as an elaborative encoding strategy."

This is part of the problem many engineers face when looking for jobs straight out of college: They've been stuck in "theory land," with little experience putting what they've learned into practice. You can run into the same issue with online learning. For example, I could spend weeks watching videos on how to set up a distributed computing system. But if I don't go to Amazon Web Services and deploy it—soon—I'll forget much of what I learned.

So whatever field you're studying, find opportunities to use your new skills. (In addition to increasing "stickiness," this also gives you a chance to discover unforeseen challenges.) Depending on the skill, you might participate in a collaborative project at work, for instance, or set up your own project on a small scale at home. Or you could find an online simulation that is similar to the real experience.

Set a golden benchmark

Just like runners in a marathon, online learners need to have a clear goal to stay focused. A return on investment (in terms of time and money spent) is hard to gauge in the near term. But those who persevere generally have their eye on a larger prize—a new job, a promotion, or the chance to lead a project. So determine a specific career objective and keep it front of mind as you learn.

Of course, that benchmark will change as you develop. Learning is a career-long process. After you achieve one big goal, set your sights on the next one. That's how you make learning a part of your normal routine. The more you do that, the less likely you are to stop.

———————

Mike Kehoe is a cofounder of BitTiger. He was formerly a consultant with Deloitte and an HR analyst at Citi.

CHAPTER 18

Talking to Yourself (Out Loud) Can Help You Learn

by Ulrich Boser

When University of Illinois psychologist Brian Ross enrolled in a computer science course, it had been a long time since he'd even taken a class. With his beard and balding dome, he stood out. A decade older than his classmates, Ross was, to all the other students, *that guy*. He was nervous.

But he had an advantage. Ross is a learning researcher, and he's familiar with the effective, but often underestimated, learning strategy known as *self-explaining*.

Adapted from content posted on hbr.org, May 5, 2017 (product #H03N5Q).

The approach revolves around asking oneself explanatory questions like, "What does this mean? Why does it matter?" It really helps to ask them out loud. A study by Dianne C. Berry shows that people who explain ideas to themselves learn almost three times more than those who don't. To help him outperform his younger colleagues, Ross asked himself lots of questions. He would constantly query himself as he read through the assigned texts. After each paragraph, after each sentence, he would ask himself: "What did I just read? How does that fit together? Have I come across this idea before?"

By the end of the course, Ross had found that, despite his relative inexperience and unfamiliarity with computers, he could answer many questions that the other students couldn't and understood programming in ways that they didn't. "I sometimes had the advantage," he told me. "I was focused on the bigger picture."

Here's how to employ self-explaining in your own learning:

Talk to yourself

Self-talk has a bad reputation; muttering to ourselves often seems to be a sign of mental distress. It's not cool to do in public. But talking to ourselves is crucial to self-explaining and generally helpful for learning. For one thing, it slows us down—and when we're more deliberate, we typically gain more from an experience.

Self-talk also helps us think about our thinking. When we're engaged in a conversation with ourselves, we typically ask ourselves questions along the lines of: "How will I know what I know? What do I find confusing?

Do I really know this?" Whether we hit the pause button while listening to a podcast or stop to reflect while reading a manual, we develop skills more effectively by thinking about our thinking.

Ask why

Self-explaining can give voice to impulses of curiosity that may otherwise remain unexplored. It's about asking ourselves the question, "Why?" Now, if we really know a topic, "why" questions are not that hard. If I asked you a why question about the town that you grew up in, the answer would come pretty easily. It's when we don't know something that why questions become more difficult—and create a way to develop an area of expertise.

To illustrate the practice, let's examine a query like "Why are there waves?" Some of us can bumble our way to a basic answer. Maybe something like "Well, waves have to do with the wind. When wind blows across the top of the water, it creates ripples of water."

But then comes the inevitable follow-up: "Why does the wind lift the water?" or "Why are there waves when there's no wind?" Here we draw a blank. Or at least I do, and so I start searching for some sort of answer, spinning through the internet, reading up on how energy moves through water. In the end, I've learned much more.

Summarize

Summarizing is a simple way to engage in self-explaining, since the act of putting an idea into our own words can promote learning.

You've probably had this experience in your own life. Recall, for instance, a time when you read an article in a magazine and then detailed its argument for a friend. That's a form of summarizing—you're more likely to have learned and retained information from that article after you did it.

The next time a person—your boss, your spouse, a friend—gives you a set of detailed instructions, take the time to verbally repeat the directives. By reciting everything back, you'll have taken steps to summarize that knowledge, and you'll be far more likely to remember the information.

Make connections

One of the benefits of self-explaining is that it helps people see new links and associations. Seeing connections helps improve memory. When we're explaining an idea to ourselves, look for relationships. That's one of the reasons that a tool like mnemonics works. We're better able to remember the colors of the rainbow because we've created a link between the first letter of the names of the colors and the acronym ROYGBIV.

When we spot links in an area of expertise, we can gain a richer understanding. This helps explain why Brian Ross had such success using self-explaining. As he learned about computer programming, he tried to explain ideas to himself, relying on different words or concepts. "A lot of what you're doing in self-explanation is trying to make connections," Ross told me. "Saying to yourself, 'Oh, I see, this works because this leads to that, and that leads to that.'"

Self-explaining should go into the learning tool kit of workers today, as the economy places new demands on making connections and adopting new insights and skills. AT&T CEO Randall Stephenson says technology workers need to learn online for at least five hours per week to fend off obsolescence. They might want to find a solitary place to do so, where they don't feel abashed about talking out loud to themselves.

———————

Ulrich Boser is a senior fellow at the Center for American Progress, where he also founded and runs the science of learning initiative. He's the author of *Learn Better: Mastering the Skills for Success in Life, Business, and School, or, How to Become an Expert in Just About Anything*.

Gain New Skills

CHAPTER 19

Make Yourself an Expert

by Dorothy Leonard, Gavin Barton, and Michelle A. Barton

"I don't know what we'd do without him!" That's what an executive in a *Fortune* 100 company recently told us about a brilliant project leader. We've heard the same sentiment expressed about many highly skilled specialists during the hundred-plus interviews we've conducted as part of our research into knowledge use and sharing. In organizations large and small, including NASA, the U.S. Forest Service, SAP, and Raytheon, managers spoke of their dependence on colleagues who have "deep smarts"—business-critical expertise, built up through

Reprinted from *Harvard Business Review*, April 2013 (product #R1304L).

years of experience, which helps them make wise, swift decisions about both strategy and tactics. These mavens may be top salespeople, technical wizards, risk managers, or operations troubleshooters, but they are all the "go-to" people for a given type of knowledge in their organizations.

Because deep smarts are mostly in experts' heads—and sometimes people don't even recognize that they possess them—they aren't all that easy to pass on. This is a serious problem, both for the organization and for those who hope to become experts themselves. Several professions build apprenticeships into their training systems. Doctors, for instance, learn on the job as interns and residents, under the close guidance of attending physicians, before practicing on their own. But the management profession has no such path. You're responsible for your own development. If you wish to become a go-to person in your organization but don't have the time or opportunity to accumulate all the experience of your predecessors, you must acquire the knowledge in a different way. The purpose of this article is to help you do just that.

A Rare Asset

Deep smarts are not merely facts and data that anyone can access. They consist of know-how: skilled ways of thinking, making decisions, and behaving that lead to success again and again. Because they are typically experience-based, deep smarts take time to develop. They are often found in only a few individuals. They are also frequently at risk. Baby boomers—some of whom have knowledge vital to their companies—are retiring in droves. And even in organizations where key experts are years from retiring, there are often only a few people with deep smarts in certain areas. If they're hired away or fall ill, their knowledge could be lost. In some fields, rapid growth or geographic expansion creates a sudden need for expertise that goes far beyond employees' years of experience. Whatever the cause, the loss or scarcity of deep smarts can hurt the bottom line when deadlines are missed, a customer is alienated, or a process goes awry.

This potential loss to the organization is an opportunity for would-be experts. Deep smarts can't be hired off the street or right out of school. High-potential employees who prove their ability to quickly and efficiently acquire expertise will find themselves in great demand.

So how do you acquire deep smarts? By consciously thinking about how the experts in your organization operate and deliberately learning from them. Of course, you can't—and don't want to—become a carbon copy of another person. Deeply smart people are unique—a product of their particular mindset, education, and experience. But you should be able to identify the elements of their knowledge and behavior that make them so valuable to the organization. For example, a colleague of the expert project leader mentioned earlier described him as an exceptional manager who could effortlessly solve any technical problem and always got the best out of his people. Initially, the colleague said he didn't know how the guy did it. But, in fact, with some prodding, he could tell us that the project leader motivated his team members by matching their roles to their interests, offering them opportunities to present to clients, and taking personal responsibility for shortfalls and mistakes, while giving others credit for progress. On the technical front, the project leader used certain identifiable diagnostic questions to understand complex issues.

The admiring colleague could have recorded and mimicked these behaviors—but he didn't. One reason, of course, is that the expert himself had never articulated his approach to project leadership. He simply recognized patterns from experience and applied solutions that had worked well in the past. It was second nature to him, like managerial muscle memory. The second stumbling block was that the colleague was accustomed to having people "push" expertise to him. That's how school and formal management-development programs work. But in today's competitive work world, that model isn't sufficient. You can't count on companies or mentors to equip you with the skills and experience you need. You must learn how to "pull" deep smarts from others.

The Right System

Let's look at a specific case, a composite drawn from the many executives we've helped to attain deep smarts:

Melissa has been with a large international beer company for more than eight years, having previously worked in a retail outlet that sold its products. She is currently a sales representative, but she has her eye on a regional VP position. In thinking about how to become more valuable to her organization (indeed, to any beverage company), she considers which in-house experts she would like to emulate. George, a general manager who has risen through the ranks from sales, is known as a smart decision maker, an outstanding negotiator, and an innovator. His colleagues say he has a remarkable ability to think both strategically and tactically about the entire business, from the brewery to the consumer, and that he balances a passion for data with in-depth talks with people in the field. In short, he would be an excellent role model.

Not everything George knows is equally valuable, of course. And Melissa does have some expertise of her own. She doesn't want to emulate George in every way. But she wishes she had his ability to evaluate, work with, and motivate the distributors who serve as the company's conduit to retailers and, ultimately, to consumers. George knows a lot about distributors because he used to work for them; he started out driving a delivery truck and made his way up the ladder before being hired by the beer company. Still, Melissa isn't going to work for a distributor; nor would it be necessary for her to experience everything George has. What she needs is to unearth the essential skills that make him so effective with distributors, internalize his insights, and mimic his critical behaviors.

Fortunately, George is willing to share his deep smarts with Melissa, but he has neither the time nor the inclination to make her training a priority. So it's up to Melissa to figure out how to learn from him. She can take two approaches, which are not mutually exclusive. She can interview George and get him to tell her stories that will provide vicarious experiences. Would-be experts who don't work alongside their role models typically need to rely on this approach. If Melissa is good at questioning, and George is able to articulate much of his knowledge, she will learn a lot. George might tell her, for instance, the story of how he first discovered the power of sales data to persuade retail store managers to display his brand of beer more prominently.

This process has limits, however. George can't tell Melissa everything he knows, because much of his wisdom is unconscious; he doesn't think about it until a particular situation calls for it. Moreover, he's often unaware of the communication style, diagnostic patterns, and body language that he uses.

How can Melissa learn these things? Through a process we call OPPTY, which stands for *o*bservation, *p*ractice, *p*artnering and joint problem solving, and *t*aking responsibilit*y*. Observation involves shadowing an expert and systematically analyzing what he or she does. Practice requires identifying a specific expert behavior or task that you can attempt on your own, but with supervision and feedback. Partnering and joint problem solving mean actively working with the expert to analyze and address challenges. Finally, when you're ready, you can take over a significant part of the expert's role. Along the way, you should deliberately reflect on each experience and internalize as much as possible.

When Melissa asks George to help her, she's careful to frame his doing so as an opportunity for both of them, since having another distribution expert at the company will mean he'll have more time to handle other issues.

She also promises to structure the knowledge sharing so that it minimizes the disruption to his heavily packed schedule.

Next, she creates an action plan that outlines her near-term and ultimate goals and the steps required to achieve them, along with suggested deadlines. (See figure 19-1.) George, and possibly his boss, will need to sign off on it.

As she goes along, Melissa notes what she has learned in a log. It's tempting to think this is unnecessary work, because we all remember very well what we've observed or done, and we assume we understand why experts behave as they do. Keeping a log forces you to check those assumptions. It serves as an accurate record of progress (allowing for the reevaluation of goals if need be) and ensures you've learned what you and the expert intended. You'll want to ask yourself questions like, What was the context of the situation? What did the expert do and why did he do it? What did I do and what feedback did I get? What worked? What didn't? What should I do next?

In the observation phase, Melissa accompanies George on his regular visits to retail stores. This takes no additional time or effort on his part but is an eye-opener for her. Before they enter the first site, George challenges her: What in the store would indicate that a top-notch distributor is serving it? She sees that he pays close attention to details such as the positioning of products in coolers, pricing relative to competitors, and even how prices are displayed. Melissa also listens when George talks with distributors, noticing how careful he is to

FIGURE 19-1

Tools for building deep smarts

Becoming an expert begins with deciding whom you will acquire knowledge from and how. Here is an excerpt from a step-by-step plan drawn up by Melissa, a high-potential sales rep in the beverage industry who aspires to become her firm's in-house whiz at distribution. Her chosen mentor is George, a general manager at her company who is the "go-to" guy in that area.

Action plan

Observation	Practice	Partner and problem solve	Take responsibility
Immediate goal: 2 months	**Short-term goal: 6 months**	**Midterm goal: 12 months**	**Ultimate goal: 24 months**
Learn how to evaluate distributors by studying retail stores they service	Learn how to evaluate our firm's performance from the distributors' point of view	Be able to diagnose problems with distributors where our sales are down, and suggest solutions	Be considered a go-to person for issues with distributors
To-do: Visit five stores with George and record what he notices.	**To-do:** Interview three distributors in region, asking about three things we do better and three things we do worse than competitors.	**To-do:** Analyze data from problem region and visit stores there. With George, visit underperforming distributors; then help him formulate a plan for addressing.	**To-do:** Take the lead on resolving conflicts between distributors and our company and let George become the backup.

speak about the broad advantages of suggested changes and to ask probing questions about operations—for example, about what incentives salespeople are given. His body language suggests empathy; he leans forward and listens intently.

After a couple of months, Melissa is ready to move on to practice what she's picked up from George. A few months after that, she begins to solve problems jointly with him. When George asks her to help analyze why a particular sales region has high sales volume but very low margins, she sees how useful it is to juxtapose data

As she puts her plan into effect, Melissa codifies her new knowledge in notes, which she later reviews and discusses with George.

Learning log

February 2011	August 2011	March 2012	April 2013
Visit to five retail stores with George	Visit to Kevan Wine & Beer, a distributor	Interview of bottom three distributors in Midwest	Creation of a task force on competing with microbreweries and craft beers. I'm the distributor liaison on this!
What happened Looked at product position in coolers, and percentage of our product there, pricing, and promotions vs. the competition. George rearranged products in the cooler! Cited stats about positioning when manager protested, and manager gave in.	**What happened** George led off: small talk, discussion of industry trends (puts guy at ease). Then he let me ask questions.	**What happened** Distributor complains that we're creating minor brands on rigid schedules, causing stockouts or oversupply (and expiration of "sell by" dates).	**What happened** Visited our distributors who are also dealing with craft beers.
Insights Store is a lens into how good the distributor is; George paid close attention to small details. See why we must go out into the field frequently—this was a good seller but could still improve.	**Insights** We have the best price points, but our ads and promotions are not as good as the competitors'. Distributor gave good feedback; could we institutionalize collecting it quarterly? Maybe build better feedback loop to ad agencies? Distributor mentioned best-selling outlet in vicinity; I should visit and find out why it's doing so well.	**Insights** Possible to schedule smaller but more-frequent batches? Rigid scheduling has ripple effect on distribution, from warehousing to delivery and merchandising in stores. Maybe top distributors have way to handle this that these underperformers don't. Need to explore by visiting more distributors and interviewing sales reps.	**Insights** Our distributors aren't good at handling so many product lines in their warehouses. Our traditional lines are suffering from less attention. Two possible options: • Help distributors move more swiftly into better automated warehouse processes. • Push for more-exclusive contracts, so distributors handle only national brands—not craft beers. Need to investigate economics and feasibility of those solutions.

analysis with visits to the field. She watches George reject a distributor's insistence on sticking with an unsuccessful strategy because it's "just the way it's always been done" and helps him brainstorm three alternative strategies for the distributor. When she reviews the learning log with George, he often comments that he rarely thinks about why he does what he does—but he agrees with her analysis.

You'll note that Melissa has both the motivation and the discipline to persevere in learning—vital requirements for this process. And George is happy to help her, which is more common among experts than you might think. Many of those we've interviewed are willing to share their knowledge—thanks to an intrinsic interest in coaching or because they have incentives to do so, such as a lightened workload, kudos from management, or the opportunity to build new knowledge and find new paths to innovation themselves.

Guided Experience

The system we outline in this article works best when aspiring experts have both time to learn and geographic proximity to the masters who will train them. However, our methods can be applied across distances and compressed in time. The U.S. Army, for example, uses parts of this process to transfer knowledge from officers serving overseas to personnel about to be deployed to the same regions. The transfer of expertise need not be one-on-one, either. An individual can accrue deep smarts from more than one expert, and an expert can mentor more than one individual.

No matter how sophisticated current technologies for data capture and analysis are, we are still highly dependent upon human skills in many situations, and such skills are best learned from experts. There is an old saying: Good judgment comes from the experience of having made bad decisions. But we believe it's more effective and efficient to build expertise through experiences guided by the smart people around you. If you observe, practice, partner, and problem solve with them before taking responsibility on your own, you'll soon become as indispensable as they are.

Dorothy Leonard is the William J. Abernathy Professor of Business Administration Emerita at Harvard Business School and chief adviser of the consulting firm Leonard-Barton Group, which conducts workshops on this and other related topics. She is the author or co-author of four Harvard Business Review Press books, including *Critical Knowledge Transfer* (Harvard Business Review Press, 2015). **Gavin Barton** is managing director of the consulting firm Leonard-Barton Group and a principal of GB Performance Consulting. He holds a doctorate from Boston University. He is the coauthor of *Critical Knowledge Transfer*. **Michelle A. Barton** is an assistant professor at Boston University School of Management and researches learning strategies during transitions and crises.

CHAPTER 20

Your Career Needs Many Mentors, Not Just One

by Dorie Clark

These days everyone knows that finding a mentor is valuable. But it's increasingly rare that we actually have one. In an in-depth study of professional service firms, Harvard Business School professor Thomas DeLong and his colleagues discovered: "Everyone we spoke with over age 40 could name a mentor in his or her professional life, but younger people often could not." They noted, "Junior professionals joining a firm 20 years ago could count on the partners treating them like protégés."

Adapted from content posted on hbr.org, January 19, 2017 (product #H03EOA).

Today, job turnover, layoffs, and increased bottom-line pressures have taken a hatchet to that "implicit agreement." The answer isn't to give up on finding a mentor, however—it's to broaden our search.

Many professionals have had success with creating mastermind groups, which are a curated mix of peers who meet regularly to discuss professional challenges and hold one another accountable. But less formal arrangements—sometimes called a mentor board of directors, a personal board of directors, or a kitchen cabinet—can also be effective.

The chief distinction between finding "a mentor" and creating "a mentor board of directors" is that there is less pressure to find one person who represents your ideal future self. You can diversify your search criteria and learn from a variety of people. This also allows you to look beyond the classic notion of a mentor as someone who is older and wiser than you.

Mentors can even be our juniors—by decades. Take Hank Phillippi Ryan, an Emmy-winning investigative reporter I profiled in my book *Reinventing You*. She launched an award-winning side career as a mystery author after being inspired by a former intern of hers who had penned a novel. "It was percolating in my head," she told me. "If she can write a book, I can write a book." To form your own mentor board of directors—stocked with an assortment of talented peers, senior professionals, and junior colleagues—keep the following questions in mind.

What, specifically, do you want to learn?

The first step in developing your board is a rigorous self-assessment. Where are you headed professionally, and what skills do you need to get there? If you're planning to shift functional roles—from sales to HR, for instance—you may want to seek out a mentor with HR experience. Similarly, if you intend to move up the management ranks, finding a mentor with great delegation skills or the ability to build relationships with difficult employees could be valuable. And don't forget about personal qualities in addition to tactical skills. The biggest game changer for you professionally may be cultivating more patience or more humility; you can seek out role models in these areas as well.

Whom do you respect most?

Once you've developed your list of skills, write down the people you know and respect who possess them. Think broadly—they could be peers, senior leaders, or even (like Phillippi Ryan's mentor) interns or junior employees. Once, when I was giving a talk on mentorship at a prominent law firm, a partner shared that early in her career, her secretary was her mentor, because the secretary, who had been at the firm for decades, understood the firm's office politics and taught her to stand up for herself. It's also useful to cast a wide net outside the office. At another mentorship workshop I conducted, one leader said that her yoga teacher was a mentor because the woman helped remind her about work-life balance.

How can you arrange to spend more time with them?

Identifying your mentor board of directors is great, but it's all hypothetical unless you actually make an effort to spend more time learning from them. For each person, think through how and when you'll create time to connect. With some of the mentors, like work colleagues, the opportunities may be plentiful. For others—a grad school professor or a former coworker who's moved to another company—you may need to think creatively. Could you invite them for a monthly lunch? Call them periodically to check in during your drive home? Arrange to meet up at a conference you'll both be attending? For each person, the opportunities (and what feels appropriate) will differ. Make a list and write down specific strategies.

How can you make the relationship reciprocal?

As with any mentor or sponsor relationship, you need to make yourself valuable in return. For each person on your list, think about what skills or qualities you bring to the table and may be able to offer them. For instance, if you're adept at social media, you could offer to help a senior professional tune up his LinkedIn profile (if he's expressed a desire to do so). Or you may have skills outside of work that your mentors value—anything from restaurant recommendations to fitness tips. For these relationships to endure, it's important to make sure they're reciprocal. That way, you're learning from each other rather than imposing on one another's time (or worrying that you're doing so).

Professional success requires a myriad of skills, knowledge, and abilities, more than we could ever hope to learn on our own. That's why mentors who can help us improve are so critical. Archetypal mentors—beneficent, all-knowing senior professionals—are in short supply these days. By updating our notions of mentorship and building a mentor board of directors, we can benefit from the knowledge of talented colleagues all around us.

———————

Dorie Clark is a marketing strategist and professional speaker who teaches at Duke University's Fuqua School of Business. She is the author of *Entrepreneurial You* (Harvard Business Review Press, 2017), *Reinventing You* (Harvard Business Review Press, 2013), and *Stand Out* (Portfolio, 2015).

CHAPTER 21

Eight Ways to Read (a Lot) More Books This Year

by Neil Pasricha

How much do you read?

For most of my adult life I read maybe five books a year—if I was lucky. I'd read a couple on vacation, and I'd always have a few slow burners hanging around the bedside table for months.

And then last year I surprised myself by reading 50 books. This year I'm on pace for 100. I've never felt more creatively alive in all areas of my life. I feel more interesting, I feel like a better father, and my writing output has

---

Adapted from content posted on hbr.org, February 3, 2017 (product #H03FGE).

dramatically increased. Amplifying my reading rate has been the domino that's tipped over a slew of others.

I'm disappointed that I didn't do it sooner.

Why did I wait 20 years?

Well, our world today is designed for shallow skimming rather than deep diving, so it took me some time to identify the specific changes that skyrocketed my reading rate. None of them had to do with how fast I read. I'm actually a pretty slow reader.

Here's my advice for fitting more reading into your own life, based on the behaviors that I changed.

Centralize reading in your home

Back in 1998, psychologist Roy Baumeister and his colleagues performed their famous "chocolate chip cookie and radish" experiment. They split test subjects into three groups and asked them not to eat anything for three hours before the experiment. Those in group 1 were given chocolate chip cookies and radishes, and were told they could eat only the radishes. Those in group 2 were given chocolate chip cookies and radishes, and were told they could eat anything they liked. Those in Group 3 were given no food at all. Afterward, the researchers had all three groups attempt to solve an impossible puzzle, to see how long they would last. It's not surprising that group 1, those who had spent all their willpower staying away from the cookies, caved the soonest.

What does this have to do with reading? I think of having a TV in your main living area as a plate of chocolate chip cookies. So many delicious TV shows tempt us, reducing our willpower to tackle the books.

Roald Dahl's poem "Television" says it all: "So please, oh please, we beg, we pray / go throw your TV set away / and in its place, you can install / a lovely bookshelf on the wall."

Last year my wife and I moved our sole TV into our dark, unfinished basement and got a bookshelf installed on the wall beside our front door. Now we see it, walk by it, and touch it dozens of times a day. And the TV sits dormant unless the Toronto Blue Jays are in the playoffs or Netflix drops a new season of *House of Cards*.

Make a public commitment

In his seminal book *Influence: The Psychology of Persuasion*, Robert Cialdini shares a psychology study showing that once people place their bets at the racetrack, they're much more confident about their horse's chances than they were just before laying down the bet. He goes on to explain how commitment is one of the big six weapons of social influence. So why can't we think of ourselves as the racehorses? Make the bet on reading by opening an account at Goodreads or Reco, friending a few coworkers or friends, and then updating your profile every time you read a book. Or put together an email list to send out short reviews of the books you read. I do that each month, with my Monthly Book Club Email. I stole the idea from bestselling author Ryan Holiday, who has a great reading list.

Find a few trusted, curated lists

The publishing industry puts out more than 50,000 books a year. Do you have time to sift through 1,000 new books a week? Nobody does, so we use proxies like Amazon reviews. But should we get our reading lists from retailers? If you're like me, and you love the "staff picks" wall in independent bookstores, there's nothing as nice as getting one person's favorite books. Finding a few trusted, curated lists can be as simple as the email lists I mentioned, but with a bit of digging you can likely find one that aligns with your tastes. Some of the reading lists that I prefer are <u>Bill Gates's, Derek Sivers's, and Tim Ferriss's list,</u> where he's collected the recommendations of many of his podcast guests.

Change your mindset about quitting

It's one thing to quit reading a book and feel bad about it. It's another to quit a book and feel proud of it. All you have to do is change your mindset. Just say, "Phew! Now I've finally ditched this brick to make room for that gem I'm about to read next." An article that can help enable this mindset is "The Tail End," by Tim Urban, which paints a striking picture of how many books you have left to read in your lifetime. Once you fully digest that number, you'll want to hack the vines away to reveal the oases ahead.

I quit three or four books for every book I read to the end. I do the "first five pages test" before I buy any book (checking for tone, pace, and language) and then let myself off the hook if I need to stop halfway through.

Take a "news fast" and channel your reading dollars

I subscribed to the *New York Times* and five magazines for years. I rotated subscriptions to keep them fresh, and always loved getting a crisp new issue in the mail. After returning from a long vacation where I finally had some time to lose myself in books, I started realizing that this shorter, choppier nature of reading was preventing me from going deeper. So I canceled all my subscriptions.

Besides freeing up mindshare, what does canceling all news inputs do? For me, it saved more than $500 per year. That can pay for about 50 books per year. What would I rather have 10 or 20 years later—a prized book collection that I've read and learned from over the years . . . or a pile of old newspapers? And let's not forget your local library. If you download Library Extension for your browser, you can see what books and ebooks are available for free right around the corner.

Triple your churn rate

I realized that for years I'd thought of my bookshelf as a fixed and somewhat artistic object: There it is, sitting by the flower vases! Now I think of it as a dynamic organism. Always moving. Always changing. In a given week I probably add about five books to the shelf and get rid of three or four. Books come in through lending libraries in our neighborhood, a fantastic used bookstore, local indie and chain stores, and, of course, online outlets. Books go out when we pass them to friends, sell them to the used bookstore, or drop them off at the lending library. This dynamism means I'm always walking over *to* the shelf, never just walking *by* it. As a result, I read more.

Read physical books

You may be wondering why I don't just read ebooks on a mobile device, saving myself all the time and effort required to bring books in and out of the house. In an era when our movie, film, and photography collections are all going digital, there is something grounding about having an organically growing collection of books in the home. If you want to get deep, perhaps it's a nice physical representation of the evolution and changes in your mind while you're reading. (Maybe this is why my wife refuses to allow my *Far Side* collections on her shelf.) And since many of us look at screens all day, it can be a welcome change of pace to hold an actual book in your hands.

Reapply the 10,000 steps rule

A good friend once told me a story that really stuck with me. He said Stephen King had advised people to read something like five hours a day. My friend said, "You know, that's baloney. Who can do that?" But then, years later, he found himself in Maine on vacation. He was waiting in line outside a movie theater with his girlfriend, and who should be waiting in front of him? Stephen King! His nose was in a book the whole time in line. When they got into the theater, Stephen King was still reading as the lights dimmed. When the lights came up, he pulled his book open right away. He even read as he was leaving. Now, I have not confirmed this story with Stephen King. But I think the message this story imparts is an important one. Basically, you *can* read a lot more. There are minutes hidden in all the corners of the day, and they add up to a *lot* of minutes.

In a way, it's like the 10,000 steps rule. Walk around the grocery store, park at the back of the lot, chase your kids around the house, and bam—10,000 steps.

It's the same with reading.

When did I read those five books a year for most of my life? On holidays or during long flights. "Oh! A lot of downtime coming," I'd think. "Better grab a few books."

When do I read now? All the time. A few pages here. A few pages there. I have a book in my bag at all times. In general, I read nonfiction in the mornings, when my mind is in active learning mode, and fiction at night before bed, when my mind needs an escape. Slipping pages into all the corners of the day adds up.

Happy reading.

———————

Neil Pasricha writes about living intentionally. He is the *New York Times*–bestselling author of six books that have sold over 1,000,000 copies, including *The Book of Awesome* and *The Happiness Equation*. He hosts the award-winning podcast *3 Books*, which is a 15-year-long quest to uncover the world's 1,000 most formative books. He gives over 50 speeches a year at places like TED, SXSW, and Harvard. Get his free articles at www.neil.blog.

CHAPTER 22

Three Ways to Use MOOCs to Advance Your Career

by Walter Frick

The vast majority of people who sign up for a MOOC—
a massive open online course—never complete it. More
than 50% consume less than half of the course's content.
This is wrongly viewed as evidence that MOOCs don't
work, that people are dropping off and not getting value.
The assumption behind that conclusion is that you have
to complete a whole, semester-long course to get value
from online education. As a MOOC addict, I can tell
you: That's not true. Instead, I've found there are at least

Adapted from content posted on hbr.org, July 26, 2016 (product #H0310I).

three good ways to learn from MOOCs, depending on your goals and the time you plan to spend.

Complete the course

In some cases, it makes sense to go for a certificate, which means completing all the coursework and usually spending money. For courses on Coursera, edX, or Udacity, getting a certificate typically requires several hours of work per week, for several weeks or even months. In the end, you get to add a line to your résumé certifying that you completed the course.

Audit the course

Another way to use MOOCs is to audit the course—watching all of the videos but not necessarily completing all of the assignments. The downside is you don't get a certificate, and in some cases you don't have full access to quizzes or other helpful materials. The upside is you have less pressure to get work done and can often learn at your own pace. In many cases, this option is also available for free.

Sample the course

Finally, in some cases you can get what you need just by sampling a MOOC, watching a video here or there to get the specific knowledge that you need. Say you wanted to do some regression modeling in Excel. Other resources may exist to learn about regression, but the instruction in MOOCs is often of higher quality. Instead of watching a full course, you might find a single lesson within a broader statistics course and watch just that lesson.

Many of the platforms will let you do this sampling for free, though others, like Lynda.com, run on a subscription basis.

How do you know which path is right for you? Here are some questions to help you decide.

Are you completely new to the topic?

If you have no background in the topic you want to learn about, taking the full course for certification is more likely to make sense. Sampling isn't a good strategy simply because you'll have a harder time deciding what it is you need to learn ahead of time. (You don't know what you don't know.) Auditing might still be an option, but the extra effort to complete the assignments will ensure that you actually learn what you hope to, and those assignments are often only available if you pay for certification.

On the other hand, if you're already somewhat familiar with the topic but need to brush up on it, auditing or sampling may make more sense. Maybe you took a marketing course in school, for instance, and maybe you intersect with the field a bit at work, but you want to refresh on the basics. Auditing a course by watching all the videos might do the trick, even if you don't complete all the assignments or pay for certification. Or, if you're trying to brush up on something narrower, seeking out and sampling a few specific videos may even be enough.

How much time can you commit?

There's a reason most people who sign up for MOOCs don't end up completing the full course, and that's because doing so takes considerable time and effort. (It also usually means spending money.)

Attempting to complete the course and receive certification only makes sense if you're sure you can spare the time. If you pay to take a MOOC, plan when you can do the work. For instance, if you commute using public transportation, you might decide to watch the videos on your way to and from work, leaving only the assignments for nights and weekends.

If you don't have several hours a week to commit, auditing or sampling will allow you to absorb the material on your own schedule.

How will you demonstrate to others what you've learned?

If you're just learning for your own enjoyment, you probably don't need to pay for a MOOC, since the main thing the money buys is certification. But if you're doing the course for work, you'll want some way to show off what you've learned.

In some cases, that's doable without certification. Maybe you can show off your new knowledge of finance by helping with your department's budget. Or if you're learning mobile app development, you can demonstrate what you've learned by building an app as a side project. If these options seem sufficient to demonstrate your skills or knowledge, you may not need to pay for the course. Alternatively, if what you're learning isn't conducive to side projects and isn't easily incorporated into your current job, paying for a certification is likely worth it.

If you choose to audit a course because you plan to demonstrate what you've learned through a side project, think ahead of time about exactly what that project will be. Be realistic. It's easy to say you'll build a website in your spare time once your course ends; in practice, you'll need to consider how you'll find the time.

There's never been more free—or nearly-free—quality educational resources available to anyone with an internet connection. Why wouldn't you find a way to use it to improve your skills and career? After all, someone else in your field surely is.

Walter Frick is a senior editor at *Harvard Business Review*.

CHAPTER 23

Should You Get an MBA?

by Ed Batista

At least once a month, an ambitious and hardworking person in their 20s asks me, "Should I get an MBA?" It's critical to determine whether your expectations for an MBA are aligned with what the degree will likely do for you. MBA programs offer three different types of benefits, all of which vary tremendously from one school to another.

Practical leadership and management skills

Management education has changed significantly over the last few decades. Previously it focused on quantitative

---

Adapted from content posted on hbr.org, September 4, 2014 (product #H00Z0H).

analysis in areas such as finance and operations, with little emphasis on other aspects of organizational life. As a result, MBAs were often seen as bean counters myopically focused on data and out of touch with the challenges managers face in the real world.

MBA programs responded by expanding their offerings in areas such as strategy, organizational behavior, and leadership. B-school curricula are still intensely quantitative, but as former Stanford Dean Garth Saloner told McKinsey, "The [quantitative] skills of finance and supply chain management and accounting and so on, I think those have become more standardized in management education, have become kind of what you think of as a hygiene factor: Everybody ought to know this."

Business schools have realized that it's not sufficient to provide only quantitative and analytical training, because within a few years of leaving school (or even immediately upon graduation), their alumni will add value more through their ability to lead and manage others than through their talents as individual contributors. And effectiveness in these more senior roles requires an entirely different interpersonal skill set. Saloner goes on to note that "the softer skill sets, the real leadership, the ability to work with others and through others, to execute, that is still in very scarce supply."

But the ability to provide quality training in these areas is unevenly distributed across MBA programs. The best schools have made leadership and interpersonal skills a high priority—Stanford now offers 12 sections of "Interpersonal Dynamics" to more than 400 students each year, making this labor-intensive course our most popular elective. Second-tier schools are making an effort to catch up, but high-caliber programs in these fields are difficult to establish. Harvard's Bill George has said, "I don't think you can *teach* leadership; I think you can *learn* about it" through experiential activities that bring students together to help them understand their strengths and limitations, and provide feedback and promote self-awareness. These activities require a very different approach from traditional lecture methods.

I'm not suggesting that the quantitative and technical skills that an MBA provides aren't useful—they absolutely are. But they're also increasingly available through other venues that individuals can access on their own at a much lower cost. The special advantage of an MBA program is the opportunity to develop leadership and interpersonal skills with a group of peers in a sequence of experiential courses informed by current research. So ask yourself:

- Do the MBA programs I'm considering provide practical leadership and management training?

- How well established are these courses? How much support do they have from the school? How much support do they have from the surrounding community?

- What do alumni say about their experiences in these courses? How have they benefited from this training?

- And what alternative means are available to me to develop these practical skills?

A credential that sends a signal to the marketplace

No career paths absolutely require an MBA—it's an optional degree and is nothing like the credentials that professions such as law and medicine make mandatory. There are many senior people in general management roles, in consulting, and even in financial services who don't have an MBA, so don't assume that the credential will necessarily serve a meaningful purpose in your chosen field.

As a coach, I have two different "markets"—my students at Stanford and my private clients, who are primarily senior leaders, and in both settings my degree sends a useful signal. New students feel more comfortable knowing that I've been in their shoes (albeit 20 years ago), and prospective clients trust that I understand the complexities of their world and the challenges they face.

But it's not a given that an MBA will have this effect. In my first job after business school, I interacted with a diverse range of communities, and while I never misled anyone about the fact that I had an MBA, I didn't advertise it either. I knew that some people in my field had negative impressions of MBAs, and I needed a chance to prove myself as an individual before being stereotyped. My particular version of this experience may have been unusual, but by no means is it unique—there are many fields and organizations in which MBAs are viewed with skepticism and even disdain.

In addition, the nature of the signal being sent depends on the specific MBA program's reputation, and this is not simply a matter of prestige. Harvard, Stanford, and Wharton routinely top lists of U.S. business schools, but they also have a reputation for entitlement and arrogance. While some firms seek out graduates from elite schools, others avoid them out of a concern that they will be difficult to work with and disruptive to the established culture. So ask yourself:

- What market am I in now? What markets might I seek to enter in the future?

- Who's interested in my services? How might this change if I had an MBA?

- How are MBAs perceived in these markets? What signals does an MBA send in these markets? What stereotypes (both positive and negative) might I face as an MBA?

- What is the specific reputation of the MBA programs I'm considering? How are these schools and their alumni viewed within my desired markets?

- And what alternative means are available to me to send the signals I desire to communicate?

Membership in a learning community and access to an alumni network

Business schools emphasize working in groups, and MBA students often learn as much from their peers as they do from faculty, so it's important to consider who you'll be working alongside for two years. Those same people will become your fellow alumni, and access to that network is one of the most valuable benefits an MBA program can offer.

Of course, alumni networks aren't created equal. Larger MBA programs yield larger networks. Certain networks are concentrated in specific geographic areas or in specific industries. And some B-school experiences create networks that are particularly active sources of mutual support.

I've benefited tremendously from the support of my fellow Graduate School of Business (GSB) alumni during two major professional transitions. In my job search after graduation and later when I began exploring executive coaching as a career path, other Stanford alumni were extraordinarily generous with their time and insights, and there's no way I could have succeeded without their help.

All this said, there's a misperception about the importance of socializing in business school as a means of cultivating these ties. To be sure, my students devote a substantial amount of time and energy to elaborate social activities, and I often find myself amused at the lengths to which they go to entertain themselves. However, while it's true that I'm middle-aged and boring, and a quiet night at home is my idea of a good time, I was pretty boring even as a student, and I didn't spend much time at parties or other social events.

But I didn't need to in order to benefit from the GSB network—the school's relatively small size and communal culture help ensure that graduates feel a sense of obligation to help fellow alumni. And the fact that I can't pay back the many people who helped me is motivation to pay it forward by doing as much as I can to support recent alumni seeking help from me. So ask yourself:

- What do I know about the students at the MBA programs I'm considering? Are they like-minded peers? Do I see myself learning alongside them?

- What do I know about the alumni networks of these programs? How active are they? Are they concentrated in geographic areas and professional fields of interest to me?

- What support does a school provide to its alumni network and to individual alumni? Do alumni return frequently to participate in events and activities at the school?

One final point on diversity: I have no doubt that my experience in business school was made substantially easier by the fact that I'm a straight, white, American man with an Ivy League undergraduate degree. Even as MBA programs have sought to attract more diverse student populations in recent years, B-schools are still disproportionately filled with people like me. And even at Stanford, which prides itself on its inclusiveness, I know that women, gays and lesbians, people of color, students from outside the United States, and non-native English speakers can feel isolated in business school and find the MBA experience more difficult and stressful. I hope to encourage people from a wide range of backgrounds to consider business school as an option, and it feels important to acknowledge this current state of affairs if anything is to change.

———————

Ed Batista is an executive coach and a lecturer at the Stanford Graduate School of Business. He writes regularly on issues related to coaching and professional development at edbatista.com, he contributed to the *HBR Guide to Coaching Employees* (Harvard Business Review Press, 2014), and is currently writing a book on self-coaching for HBR Press. Follow him on Twitter @edbatista.

Move Ahead, Move Up

CHAPTER 24

You Don't Need a Promotion to Grow at Work

by Jordan Stark and Katie Smith Milway

As organizations run leaner and flatter, your ability to move up can stall much earlier in your career because, simply put, there's no place to go. This is true whether you work for a corporation, nonprofit, or public agency. So what should you do when you reach that plateau and you're only midway through your career? First, take stock. Do you enjoy and learn from your colleagues? Are you still energized by the mission of the organization? If the answer is no, it may be time to move on. But if the answer is yes, consider ways to grow on the plateau.

Adapted from content posted on hbr.org, June 24, 2015 (product #H026BW).

There are at least four proven approaches, all of which require that you ask what energizes you and what saps your motivation.

Make a lateral move

Lateral moves within your organization can be a great way to build new skills and relationships and get exposure to different products or services. You can explore new internal opportunities in a few ways, by conducting internal informational interviews and meeting with a leader in another division or unit; taking on cross-cutting assignments involving other business units; or volunteering to move, say, from a business unit to a staff function that transcends units, such as finance, HR, or operations. Indeed, corporations like Kraft consider role rotation standard for building well-rounded leaders, and actively invite promising line managers to take on staff jobs and the reverse. One senior leader at a professional services company, whom we'll call Bronwyn, made the move from client-facing partner to chief operating officer. She was able to build on the analytics and change management insights she had brought to clients to help strengthen her own organization from the C-suite. In the process, she developed managerial muscle in finance, human resources, governance, and IT, and, as a bonus, Bronwyn gained more flexibility in her schedule since she didn't have external client demands driving her day-to-day work.

Reshape your role

Reshaping your current role is another way to grow on the plateau. This calls for taking inventory of what you'd like to do more of, less of, and start doing. In concert with team members, you can redraw some boundaries to create stretch opportunities for others as you shift responsibilities to make space for your own new challenges. Two good places to look for these challenges are on your supervisor's plate (does she have areas of responsibility that you find interesting and could help free her up?); and in employee and customer surveys (are there needs the organization isn't meeting that you have the skills to respond to?) An expert in customer strategy at a consumer products company, whom we'll call Sandra, became a vice president in her early 30s and knew that she would need to wait a while for her next promotion, given the company's culture. She knew she wanted to stay with the company, however, so she looked for gaps in service delivery across business units—from supply chain to e-commerce—and then volunteered to help colleagues fill those gaps. Sandra spent the next several years intrapreneurially expanding activities within her vice president role, learning more about the company and gaining new skills, relationships, and a reputation for innovation.

Expand your influence

Expanding your influence through actively mentoring others, building internal communities of practice, or stepping up to represent your organization with external bodies can forge satisfying new frontiers without changing roles. Take the program officer at a youth-focused nonprofit whom we'll call Maria. She had nowhere to move up internally unless the executive director moved on. So she began collaborating externally with other organizations in her city that aimed to help immigrant youth plug into education, training, and job opportunities, growing her network and innovating her programs. By expanding her influence outside the organization, she gained credibility within. When the time finally came to name a new executive director, Maria was a top internal candidate in part because of her external network, and eventually got the job.

Deepen your skills

Deepening your skills is another way to build credibility and opportunity on the plateau. You can accomplish this on the job, by seeking out a mentor or volunteering for special projects, and off the job through formal leadership training. A medical service head we'll call Robert, at a large public hospital, volunteered to lead a performance improvement exercise for one of the hospital's acute care groups. The results in improved patient care and timelier billing led hospital management to invest in sending him to an executive education course at a top business school, a qualification that eventually garnered him an offer to run a much bigger service line at the hospital, with close to 300 medical staff and a $380 million annual budget.

Most 21st-century managers will find themselves on a similar plateau somewhere along their career. Before succumbing to the temptation to jump to a new escarpment, consider whether branching out in place may be the best way to build your skills, both personally and professionally, for your next ascent.

Jordan Stark is a partner and executive coach at Next Step Partners. **Katie Smith Milway** is a senior advisor at The Bridgespan Group and principal of Milway Consulting.

CHAPTER 25

Position Yourself for a Stretch Assignment

by Claudio Fernández-Aráoz

I once hired a McKinsey consultant for a country manager role in a developing region. Two years later, despite great success, he told me he wanted to find a job at another company in his home country. I could see he was motivated, and still eager to grow, so I pushed him to instead think about what larger global roles he could perform for his current employer. He did and was soon appointed to manage the company's entire international business from headquarters. It was a stretch assignment for him, but one in which he has thrived.

Adapted from content posted on hbr.org, March 27, 2012.

Companies everywhere, in nearly every industry, can struggle to fill their talent pipelines. As a result, many organizations—like the one in the story above—are willing to consider candidates—like that country manager—who aren't a perfect fit for a particular role now, but who could be soon. They're willing to give people stretch assignments, which presents a huge opportunity for ambitious job-seekers. So how do you position yourself to take advantage of the situation? Ask the following questions.

Do you really have what it takes?

To win and succeed in a stretch assignment, high potentials need to have the right motive (a willingness to have an impact on others in a selfless way), the right leadership assets (including, among others, the ability to learn, stay resilient, and connect), and be willing to accept the costs of a senior executive position.

Is it the right opportunity?

Not all stretch assignments are created equal. Here are a few things to consider:

- Moving within a company tends to work better than switching to a different one. You will fit more easily into the culture, retain part of your social capital, and have larger chances to recover if you fail.

- Short-term projects are a good way to stretch without committing to a permanent change. Consider starting small projects even without a mandate.

- Although it's important to explore the parts of the organization you know best, the most meaningful stretch assignments are the ones that push you not just into more responsibility but into more cross-cultural collaboration (whether it's working across units, functions, or geographies). This is a key competence for global leaders.

- Challenge yourself just enough. The sweet spot of development for high achievers is when you have a 50% to 70% chance of success.

- You can't do it alone. Choose a trusted adviser to help you confirm your true strengths, and decide who you want to be, what assignment to look for, and how to get it.

How can you get it?

Assuming you have what it takes, and the assignment is right, here are some tips for securing it:

- Choose the right sponsor. Identify the executive with the best mix of power and credibility to put you forward for the job, and openly share your ambitions.

- Explain very clearly why you should get the assignment. Demonstrate that you have the competence required, even if your previous experience doesn't look too relevant. For example, a track record of effectively working across functions or units may be a relevant indicator of your ability to work in a larger global role.

- Plan and discuss your integration. Understand the key challenges and conditions for success, including internal communication and resources. Define a realistic timetable for objectives, including learning, building relationships, and scoring early wins.

- Be prepared to work very hard. Succeeding in a stretch assignment requires a huge commitment—only proportional to the eventual reward.

Claudio Fernández-Aráoz is a senior adviser at the global executive search firm Egon Zehnder, an executive fellow at Harvard Business School, and the author of *It's Not the How or the What but the Who* (Harvard Business Review Press, 2014).

CHAPTER 26

Having the Here's-What-I-Want Conversation with Your Boss

by Rebecca Shambaugh

One person stands between you and your next raise or promotion: your boss. While others on the leadership team—and even your peers—may exert some influence on your career future, it's your direct supervisor who can pull the strings to either grant or deny your chance for advancement. But to get what you want, you have to ask for it.

Adapted from content posted on hbr.org, November 20, 2015 (product #H02IBL).

Despite this truth, research from the Society of Human Resource Management has found that the majority of people—nearly 80%—feel uncomfortable discussing salary and other employment terms.

After I spoke at a conference in New York, a female executive pulled me aside to ask my advice on this topic. She explained that while she was on the verge of being promoted to the C-suite, her family situation with three children had many demands. She was feeling conflicted about whether or not she could take on higher-level responsibilities while remaining both a strong professional and strong parent. In confidence, she shared with me that she was planning to resign from her position and company later that month. I then asked her, "Did you consider going to your boss and directly asking for what you wanted—maybe some additional time off or even going part-time for a while—to facilitate your ability to accept the promotion while still making more time for family?" My point was based on the fact that when it comes to your career, whether it involves a promotion, a raise, or another goal, it doesn't have to be all or nothing—*if* you learn how to identify what you want and then confidently ask for it.

At its core, the act of asking your superior for something important to your career progression may make you feel vulnerable, yet summoning the courage to ask to do so actually demonstrates strength. Whether you seek more money, higher status, increased visibility, additional resources, or more time off, you likely won't get it if you don't specifically ask your boss for it. What's more, when it comes to achieving the next step up in pay, position, or preferences, many bosses *expect* you to ask for what you want directly. Asking shows both self-confidence and respect for your boss by acknowledging that you're requesting, not just expecting, help.

Assuming that you've already done your prep work—researching your case, and your company's policies and financial position—here are a few tips on actually having that conversation with your boss.

Avoid assumptions by asking the right questions

Successful negotiation is not just about being willing to ask for what you want, but approaching your "ask" strategically. A poor strategy is approaching negotiations one-dimensionally, focusing only on your own desired outcomes. Instead, you should take a collaborative approach, building a clear bridge between your boss's concerns and your request. The best way to do this is to prepare to pose a few open questions that explore your boss's view of the world. When formulating these questions, be curious about how to make your request a win-win. For example, you might try using phrases that imply joint success, such as:

- "How do we both do well?"

- "How would you define success?"

- "How can we turn this into a win for you?"

However, when keeping your boss's perspective in mind, be careful not to spend too much time listening passively, or go overboard with the questioning. The key is to find the perfect balance between listening and asking questions, ultimately steering the discussion toward an answer.

Gather context through open dialogue

Getting the lay of the land directly from your manager before asking for what you want can help you formulate a better strategy. Initiate an open dialogue tailored to the specific points you plan to soon negotiate. For example, if you're targeting a promotion, you might ask something like this:

- "Now that I've been in this role for two years, what actions would it take to advance to the next level?"

This type of question can open the door to the possibility of your boss revealing valuable information to guide your future negotiation. For example, your boss may tell you that there is currently a freeze on promotions, but it's an avenue that can be explored in six months. In this case, you'll then know that the timing is wrong to negotiate for a promotion right now, so you can shift gears to ask for something else, or pose other questions to help you gather the information you need to improve your chances of getting what you want down the road. For example, some questions you might next ask include:

- "Assuming things are different six months from now, what are my chances of gaining a promotion?"

- "What specifically do I need to do to achieve this goal?"

- "Are there stretch assignments that I can take on over the next six months to prepare me for advancement?"

Then follow your boss's guidance and commit to revisiting the topic in six months for a reevaluation of the timing.

Use "what if" responses

One way to build on your boss's responses during the open dialogue stage is to have some "what if" responses ready to go. What-if responses give you a way to further the conversation by suggesting specific actions that you might take when your boss makes a general suggestion. For example, if your boss says that you need more cross-functional experience before you can advance, you might reply with an exact strategy that you could implement to get that experience such as:

- "What if I work directly with the marketing department on the Johnson campaign?"

- "What if I take the lead in sharing our communications strategy with the sales team?"

- "What if I shadow the distribution team lead for a week, or participate in a one-day role swap with a peer in the finance department?"

Involving your boss in your request using the what-if tactic will help gain his or her buy-in and commitment with a tangible plan that can be tracked and monitored.

Let the conversation evolve

Even if you execute a perfect ask, there may be circumstances beyond your control that cause your boss to reject your request. Don't become so fixated on achieving your ultimate goal that you leave possible chips on the table. Keep an eye out for viable backup plans that emerge as the conversation unfolds. Even if you get a no response to your original request, you can still leave the negotiation with a small win that may put you on the path to an eventual yes. Your goal should be to avoid ending up in a position where the response is a final no.

For example, if you ask for a salary bump, proving through your internal and external market research why you deserve one, yet your boss responds that there's no budget for raises in the department currently, you might shift the conversation to requesting an extra week of vacation, more flexibility in your job, a benefit option, or paid continuing education in an area that supports your career goals.

Even if you accept a Plan B as a result of your current negotiation with your boss, that's no reason to give up completely on what you really want. If your manager denies your request the first time, it doesn't necessarily mean that no is the final answer.

No matter your perceived level of expertise in negotiation or which style you use to go about it, there is power in simply moving beyond your nervousness and starting a conversation with your boss about what you want. By doing so, you'll begin to build both your skill level and confidence, preparing you for future negotiations.

While you may not get what you want every time, if you don't ask, you'll never know.

Rebecca Shambaugh is an internationally recognized leadership expert, author, and keynote speaker. She's president of SHAMBAUGH, a global leadership development organization, and founder of Women In Leadership and Learning (WILL).

CHAPTER 27

How to Ask for a Promotion

by Rebecca Knight

Asking for a promotion can be nerve-racking. But when you think you're ready for the next step, it's important to say so. How do you prepare for that conversation with your boss? What information should you have at the ready? And how exactly do you make your case?

What the Experts Say

"Asking for a promotion makes you feel vulnerable," says Sabina Nawaz, a CEO coach, leadership keynote speaker, and writer. "You're not in control; you're putting yourself in the hands of your manager to be judged—and you

---

Adapted from content posted on hbr.org, January 29, 2018 (product #H044IV).

might be judged not worthy." You may fret that you'll be "bugging your boss" or come across as greedy and "self-serving." But, to advance in your career, you'll need to learn to advocate for yourself, says Joseph Weintraub, the founder and faculty director of the Babson Coaching for Leadership and Teamwork Program. "You can't assume that the organization will take care of you just because you do a good job," he says. "There is a degree of self-promotion that's needed." Put simply: "If don't you ask, you don't get." Here are some pointers on how to make the request.

Reflect

The first step in the process, is to think through what you want, Weintraub says. "Do you want more power? More money? More managerial responsibility?" Is there already a position you covet, or do you wish to create a new role? Do you want to move up—or might a lateral move interest you? It's also important to "think about your skill set and how it aligns with the objectives of the organization," he says. This will help you position your promotion request in a way that connects to broader strategic goals.

Do Some Research

It's smart to gather outside intelligence too, says Nawaz. "The more senior you get, the more likely it is that your promotion is not the sole decision of your manager," she notes. "Your manager's peers have input as well." She recommends "soliciting feedback from a personal board of directors" on your strengths and weaknesses, and speaking to peers to try to "gauge your institutional reputation." The past is precedent. Find out how others successfully pressed their cases for promotion. This might help you uncover effective strategies. Also ask your colleagues how they perceive your promotion readiness. And, when it comes to granting your request, "it's not just the business results [that matter]. You have to be someone that people are willing to follow."

Build Your Case

Once you've clarified exactly what you're looking for, build a compelling case for why you deserve to move up. This is particularly important if you're asking to advance ahead of your organization's promotion cycle. Be prepared for a "what-have-you-done-for-me-lately mentality," says Nawaz. She recommends preparing a one- or two-page memo that "clearly outlines your proven track record." The memo's bullet points ought to "provide concrete metrics of the impact you've had," descriptions of "solutions you've delivered," and financial outcomes for which you've been responsible. It might also include "data from other divisions or consumer or employee surveys" that point to your success. "You're trying to prove that you're already working at the level you're asking to be promoted to," she says. Weintraub also recommends thinking about "who your successor might be" at this stage and figuring out how to champion that colleague. Show your manager that "you're working hard to develop someone else," he says. "This not only showcases your leadership capabilities; it will also relieve your boss to know that there is someone who can fill your shoes."

Consider Timing

There's no perfect time to ask for a promotion, but you should be savvy about when you make the request, says Weintraub. Obviously, the week after a round of layoffs at the company or the day your team loses a key client isn't ideal. Instead, ask "after something good has happened." Perhaps you've just signed a major new deal or your company announced a solid earnings quarter. Nawaz agrees: "When there's a lot of churn happening, it might be the best thing to jump in, roll up your sleeves, and simply do the work to stabilize the organization." On the other hand, don't be lulled into complacency. If your promotion will help the company achieve its objectives, press on.

Plant the Seed

Asking for a promotion is not a one-and-done discussion; rather, it's a series of continuing conversations, says Nawaz. Using your memo as a guide, she recommends that "your early words should be something along the lines of: 'I am excited to be here and to make an impact. Here is the impact I've already made. I would like to have ongoing discussions with you about what it would take for me to get to the next level.'" Weintraub recommends "framing the conversation around excellence," while making your reasons for wanting a promotion clear. "There's that old adage that managers do things right and leaders do the right things," he says. "Tell your boss: 'I want to make sure that what I'm doing is not just good, but excellent.'" Then ask: What can I do to make you confident that I'm ready for the next step? "Demonstrate your willingness to grow and learn," he says.

Nurture the Seed

Once you've planted the seed, "nurture it over time," says Nawaz. She recommends asking your manager for feedback "not so often that it becomes an irritant, but, say, every month or every quarter." Be specific. If, for instance, your promotion involves more client-facing responsibilities, she suggests saying something like: "I've spent the past month talking with our key enterprise clients and here's what I've learned. What feedback do you have for me?" Another smart strategy, according to Weintraub, is to present your boss "with ideas of how you would spend your first 90 days on the job." "Show you've done your homework and that you're serious about" earning a promotion.

Don't Be Reckless

Using an outside offer to get a promotion can work—and often does. If nothing more, an outside job offer builds your confidence and gives you more information about your market worth. (This is particularly pertinent if your primary reason for wanting a promotion is financial.) But as a strategy to get your boss on your side, it comes with many risks. "Promotion by hostage is not a good way to win friends and influence people," says Weintraub. "People generally don't respond well to ultimatums." Nawaz echoes the sentiment. This tactic often has a "negative impact on relationships" and "artificially promotes people who are not ready to be promoted" in the first place, she says. "Be very careful about playing this card."

Be Patient (to a Point)

It would be great if your boss agreed to promote you on the spot, "but don't count on it happening," says Nawaz. Promotions rarely happen overnight, and you mustn't get discouraged if you don't immediately succeed. "Be realistic," she says. While you're waiting, "continue to do good work, sincerely look for ways to increase your impact, and elevate the level at which you operate." That said, don't ignore signs that things may not be going your way. "If you look around and see others getting promotions that you're not getting, talk to your boss," says Weintraub. "Say: 'Will you recommend me for a promotion when one becomes available?'" If you learn that you're "not on your manager's short list," then "think about whether you want to stay in your organization or look for a job elsewhere." The bright side: "At least you know."

Case Study: Create a "Résumé of Accomplishments" to Bolster Your Argument

Earlier in her career, Gretchen Van Vlymen—then an HR manager at a company in Chicago—decided she was ready to ask her boss for a promotion.

Her first step was determining the role she wanted: "I looked at where there were gaps in the company that need to be filled," says Gretchen. "I knew that if I could connect my own career path to the company's overarching goals, it would make my promotion more compelling for upper management."

After a period of reflection, she zeroed in on a new role: VP of HR. The job would involve managing the HR team, and also recruiting and hiring for the company itself.

Before talking to her boss, Gretchen created a "résumé of accomplishments," which included numerous examples that demonstrated how she'd mastered the responsibilities associated with her role and was ready for the next move. For example, she described how she revised the company's internal handbook by using skills she honed as a consultant and crowd-sourcing HR ideas from the team she already managed. (The handbook was rolled out companywide.)

"I [wanted to showcase] ways in which I had added to the organization by going above and beyond what was required of my current job," she says. "I also wanted to show how those efforts affected the productivity of my team and department—and consequently the [company's] bottom line."

Gretchen also devised a game plan for how her team would manage, should her promotion be granted. "I made a list of duties that I could easily transition to the team members I had trained," she says.

She then set up a meeting to talk to her boss. "I was clear and concise while outlining the prep from my 'résumé,'" she says.

Gretchen made sure to say she was "realistic about timing" for the move. And, indeed, her boss didn't say yes right away. In fact, he had some specific concerns.

"He posed tough questions about how I could make time for new responsibilities when my plate was already full," she says.

She left the meeting with a promise from him that he would revisit the issue over the coming months. "In the meantime, he challenged me with several short-term goals."

Gretchen was successful. She received her promotion, and today she is the VP of HR at Stratex, an HR services company.

———————

Rebecca Knight is a freelance journalist in Boston and a lecturer at Wesleyan University. Her work has been published in the *New York Times*, *USA Today*, and the *Financial Times*.

CHAPTER 28

Learn to Get Better at Transitions

by Avivah Wittenberg-Cox

There is a small, disheveled baby robin making her very first steps in my garden today. She looks a bit dazed and exhausted, her lovely yellow down all awry. I know exactly what she feels like. She looks like a lot of people I know right now. At almost every age, everyone seems to be on the cusp of a similar transition: taking their first steps into an uncertain and illegible new world. As I write this, World War II planes fly overhead to celebrate Queen Elizabeth's official birthday. Like my own mother, who shares her birthday, she is turning 93. They are both remarkably well, and not finished with transitions.

Adapted from content posted on hbr.org, July 5, 2018 (product #H04FD4).

At just shy of 57, I feel poised between these two ends of the spectrum, the baby bird and the great-grandmother. From this middle spot, I can observe my entire family hanging, in a seemingly collective cliff ritual, on the edge of change. We are all transitioning—quasi-simultaneously and quite unexpectedly—into our next chapters. My daughter is graduating from college. My son is starting his first company. My husband is adapting to something he resists calling retirement. My mother has just been fitted with her first hearing aids and is suddenly complaining about the noise of the sirens in the city. Not to mention my trio of good friends, one who lost a job, one who moved to another country, and one who split from her partner.

Every one of this cross-generational crew is struggling to let go of *what was* (identity, community, colleagues, and competencies) to embrace what's next (as yet unknown, undefined, and ambiguous). There is a mixture of fear (*Who am I?*) and excitement (*I am SO ready for a change*), confusion (*What do I want?*) and certainty (*Time to move on*).

Because more of us are living longer, healthier lives, we'll face more of these moments of liminality. And so I'm sitting in the garden, watching Robin Jr. test her fledgling wings, researching how to prepare for the several decades still ahead. No matter where we are in our own journeys, we could all get better at the skill of transitioning. To do this, focus on four component skills.

Pacing and planning

Longevity means that, more than ever, we need to plan for change. Using the gift of decades requires acknowledging their existence and deciding what you want to do with them. People say you can't have it all, but the gift of time gives us new options to have a lot more than we ever thought possible.

- Measure out your life to date in major chapters. Erik Erikson mapped out adulthood in seven-year periods. What were the highlights, accomplishments, and learnings of each of your past seven-year periods?

- How many seven-year periods do you have before you hit 100?

- Draw a timeline from 0 to 100 and place yourself on it. This gives you an idea of the possible length of the road ahead.

Leaving gracefully

There comes a time in jobs, life phases, or relationships where you know an arc has reached its end. Knowing when it is time to end—and ending well—will become an increasingly valuable skill as lives lengthen and transitions become multiple across both personal and professional lives. Ends can come from within, the result of burnout or boredom, depression or exhaustion. Or they can come from without, the land of restructurings and layoffs, divorce or other major life shifts. They are the prequel to re-creation. It is not always an easy time—for anyone involved, at work or at home. We can spend quite a lot of it loitering unproductively, wondering whether we should stay or go. But good endings are the best building blocks to good beginnings.

- Choosing to choose gives you agency. The choice itself, sometimes made years before you actually move, is the first, and often the biggest, step.

- Ask yourself if you are staying where you are out of love, or out of fear. Do you love where you are, or do you fear leaving it for a murky unknown? The latter is a lousy place from which to live, but many of us stay stuck here. *Who would I be without this title, this salary, or this position?* It can be an exciting question, not a scary one.

- Embrace confusion, ambiguity, and questions. There redefinition lies. And remember, you don't have to face them alone.

Letting the inside out

Self-knowledge is one of the hard-won rewards of aging. For many of us, our inner selves remain unexplored territory until the second half of adulthood. My friend Mary had yearned for creative outlets much of her life but had never considered herself artistic until she took up writing and painting in her sixties. At 80, she is a successful artist and published poet. What part of yourself might be waiting, hidden in the wings? A few questions to set you on your way:

- What have you most enjoyed in your career to date?

- What kinds of people energize you, and what kinds of environments shut you down?

- Do you want to transfer skills or start from scratch and reinvent? Build on accomplishments or never hear of them again?

- What kind of balance will you prioritize for this phase? Focus on one thing or cumulate a series of side-hustles into a portfolio life?

- Do you want to anchor security or toss it to the winds?

In this journey, which can take a few years, you'll want to pack a comforting "travel bag": an advisory board of trusted supporters, a realistic timeline, a financial plan, and clearly negotiated support from your partner, if you have one. Preparing for the next third of your life requires more than updating your LinkedIn profile. Invest in the next phase as you would in any seven-year project. Seriously.

Letting the outside in

Any transition plan will benefit from feedback from the outside world. Essentially, you're market testing your new plan, and figuring out where you're most needed and appreciated. Clare and Mark thought that when they reached their early sixties, they'd retire and leave their U.K. base to live in a new country. So, in their fifties, they took a sabbatical from work and lived in four different countries for three months each to find the perfect place. In the end, this experience helped them decide to enter a new profession instead of a new country. They decided to move to a new home just an hour from where they'd been living and start an eco-friendly farm, fulfilling a long-held passion for sustainability and food.

This is a process London Business School professor Herminia Ibarra calls "outsight"—actually visiting these metaphorical new lands to discover not only what you love but where you are loved. Her point is that insight alone may not be enough:

- What do others most appreciate about you?

- What have you done or worked on that elicits the best response, the most appreciation, or follow-up?

- Which of your experiments have attracted the kind of questions, people, or projects that excite you?

- When, where, and with whom did you feel most alive?

Leaping

Seeing people who have transitioned successfully to a new phase and invested in something they deeply care about, sometimes for the first time in their lives, is an inspiring sight. Some people only really find, or allow themselves to find, their calling after they've fulfilled all their duties—to their own earlier expectations, to parents, to family. The freedom that comes from finally aligning with yourself is profound. Neither fame nor fortune can feed the unsatisfied soul. As Erich Fromm wrote half a century ago, "The whole life of the individual is nothing but the process of giving birth to himself; indeed, we should be fully born when we die—although it is the tragic fate of most individuals to die before they are born."

Now that we have a few extra decades to test our wings, the real challenge may be remembering that it's never too late to fly.

———————

Avivah Wittenberg-Cox is CEO of 20-first, one of the world's leading gender consulting firms, and author of *Seven Steps to Leading a Gender-Balanced Business* (Harvard Business Review Press, 2014).

Index

Engage with HBR content the way you want, on any device.

With HBR's new subscription plans, you can access world-renowned **case studies** from Harvard Business School and receive **four free eBooks**. Download and customize prebuilt **slide decks and graphics** from our **Visual Library**. With HBR's archive, top 50 best-selling articles, and five new articles every day, HBR is more than just a magazine.

Subscribe Today
hbr.org/success

Smart advice and inspiration from a source you trust.

If you enjoyed this book and want more comprehensive guidance on essential professional skills, turn to the HBR Guides Boxed Set. Packed with the practical advice you need to succeed, this seven-volume collection provides smart answers to your most pressing work challenges, from writing more effective emails and delivering persuasive presentations to setting priorities and managing up and across.

Harvard Business Review Guides

Available in paperback or ebook format. Plus, find downloadable tools and templates to help you get started.

- Better Business Writing
- Building Your Business Case
- Buying a Small Business
- Coaching Employees
- Delivering Effective Feedback
- Finance Basics for Managers
- Getting the Mentoring You Need
- Getting the Right Work Done

- Leading Teams
- Making Every Meeting Matter
- Managing Stress at Work
- Managing Up and Across
- Negotiating
- Office Politics
- Persuasive Presentations
- Project Management

HBR.ORG/GUIDES

Notes

Strengths	Weakreses
	perfectionism →too detailed

enthusiastic
about lifelong
learning
	• activation
	  energy
	  fix by
	  habits

• focus ◉	

Ch 21 To Read more Books

○ Have a Book on me at all
                                    times
○ Always read , while
     waiting in line ... etc.
• Follow reading lists: | Try
      Bill Gates | podcast:
      Tim Ferris | 3 Books

Pg 218

Now that I've been at this role
for close to 3 mounth, ...

     what are my
         Chances of getting a
         full time offer

You've gave me complex
→ that I've hand us asignmeet

Notes

Notes

Notes

Notes

Notes

Notes

Notes

Notes

Notes

Notes

Notes

Notes

Notes